ONE SURVIVOR'S STORY

THE POWER *to* CHOOSE

SUSAN M. BISAHA

Published in the United States by
Susan M. Bisaha Publishing
Ocean Grove, New Jersey

Book design and layout by Studio 325.

ISBN 978-0-692-58422-4
Printed in the United States of America.

ACKNOWLEDGMENTS

This book would not have been possible without the following people:

My wonderful wife, Kate, who for over twelve years has been my constant support and cheerleader. Thank you honey, for enduring incredible lows and celebrating magnificent highs. Thank you for literally picking me up and encouraging me to move forward. I love you!

My brother and sister, who for decades have helped me through this journey. Thank you both for always believing me and believing "in me." I love you!

My amazing brother-in-law and sister-in-law, Lou and Jeanine and their children Jenn, Lauren, Emily, Ryan and Oat. You guys ARE my family.

My dear friends both past and present: Lorraine, Marie, Rachel, Doris, Janice, Karen, Diane, Mo, Marge, Jeannie, Julie, Santa, Harriet, Carole and Wendy: You crazy beautiful women have shown me that laughter is healing and that love can be pure and safe. Thank you all for loving me for all the right reasons!

My friend and guide, Lorraine Moore. Thank you for giving me clear vision and understanding of my life's work. You have blessed me more than I can say!

Melissa Marici, with The Marketing House. Thank you for steering me in the right direction and giving me countless hours of time and support. I appreciate you!

My design team at Studio325. You MADE this book! Thank you for your talent and enthusiasm in making my book a reality. You are wonderful and so very talented!

Dr. Sandy Goldstein, Teri, and the staff of Convery Dental Associates. Thank you for taking care of me emotionally as well as physically for over forty years. Your genuine kindness has been a true gift!

Dr. Louis Bersalona and the staff of Seaview Medical Associates. Your gentle compassionate care has been a blessing in my life. Thank you for your humanness and kindness. I am profoundly grateful for you!

My hundreds of clients past and present. EACH and EVERY one of you has inspired me to be a better therapist and has assured me that there is a brilliant light at the end of every tunnel. Thank you all for trusting me and allowing me into your lives.

And finally, my Mom and Dad. You gave me life, love, and the profound gift of telling me I was wanted. I am so proud to be your daughter! Wherever you are in the cosmos, I hope you are laughing, dancing, visiting old friends, and promoting my book! Come on, Mom...I know you are knocking down doors right now!

CONTENTS

INTRODUCTION

It was not my plan to write hundreds of pages about my life. I was prouder than a peacock when I presented, ""my story;" a whopping twenty-five pages to various publishers and literary agents, certain I would soon have book in hand. When the rejections kept coming and coming, I was perplexed; hurt and pissed, but mainly perplexed. "This is such a great story," I thought. "It is so important and can help so many." I kept giving the positive energy to the Universe and kept waiting...and waiting. Nothing. Then on a weekend trip to Connecticut, the Universe gave me an unexpected gift. While in a Goodwill Store parking lot, my sister-in-law Jeanine saw a good friend. She and Melissa chatted as Kate and I stood by, waiting to be introduced. We were cordial; nothing of great substance. Later on while chatting at the house, I asked Jeanine what Melissa did for a living (something I usually could care less about when I meet someone in a parking lot). "She's a literary agent," Jeanine said. Kate and I looked at each other with raised eyes and a hopeful stare. Jeanine knew I had written a manuscript many months before, but I had not shared my plethora of rejections with family or friends. Call it superstition or just plain shame. I asked Jeanine for Melissa's contact information and after several texts and brief conversations, we met at a unique eatery in Brookfield to discuss how to share my story with the world.

The day after meeting with Melissa, I was up at the crack of dawn. Actually, that's not entirely true; I did not sleep at all. When I formally got out of bed it was pitch dark with a faint rustling of our cats around the house. I bumped into the living room sofa and proceeded to the kitchen where they get that first meal of the day. I feed them every morning around the same time, but this particular morning was much earlier... much. As I began doling out the goodies, I caught them staring at me with this look on their faces...as if to say, "What the f...ck are you doing here so early?" Good question with an easy answer. When we met with Melissa, she told me I needed to develop my story...let the reader into my intimate journey, my core thoughts and feelings. I needed to give a lot more. All night I lay in bed wondering how to do that. I needed to fill up hundreds of pages about...well...me. Why? Why put myself through this regurgitation of the past? Who would read it anyway? My thoughts turned into a stomachache which manifested a headache which initiated my formally getting out of bed so early in the first place (my wife was pleased, by the way!). The cat feeding continued with our outside colony of catch-and-release guys. They, as well as our inside guys, usually were fed later in the morning, but since they spotted me inside rustling around the dark house and were tracking my every move through the kitchen window, I had to commit. I gathered their food and proceeded outside in the darkness. After putting down their morning meal, I stood up and stood still. I was completely overwhelmed and started to cry; I lost it. Right at that moment, I looked up at the completely empty sky and saw one brilliant bright star; at least I think it was a star, but let's not ruin the moment! I stopped dead in my tracks, looking up and admiring this isolated wonder of the universe. It was me. It was my thoughts about myself for decades as well as my thoughts and fears now; isolated...bright and important, yet all alone in the world. My panic of "I can't" suddenly changed to "I am." I am as bright and shining and important and valuable and luminous as that one star. I am allowing my past to lift me up instead of tear me down. I walked back into the house and stared at my parents' wedding photo. Both so young and alive. Both gazing into my eyes. I wanted so much for them to jump off the page and talk to me. "Tell me I can do this," I repeated to this fifty-year-old piece of photo paper. Nothing. I took a deep breath and said out loud, "What should I do?" To this day, I cannot explain what happened. Call it a combination of calmness and determination. Call it a peaceful fire. Call it knowing. "Oh yeah," I said out loud, "I got this."

CHAPTER ONE

IN THE BEGINNING...

It's hard to think of life before life. Many believe we have lived countless times before in many shapes and sizes. And we keep doing so in order to learn and to grow. All I know is mine felt like a wicked wild struggle from the beginning. My very first memory is when I was two. It was my sister's christening. My father, brother and I were standing outside of an old Catholic church in Perth Amboy, NJ while my baby sister was being baptized. Dad must have taken us outside for some air and probably to let off some steam. My brother was a couple of years older than me. I remember staring up at this big statue of the Blessed Virgin Mary (that's Catholic for those who don't know) that had a concrete circular base about a foot wide. The statue seemed a hundred feet tall to a pipsqueak like me. I remember my brother boosting himself up onto the base of the statue and walking round and round. He looked so confident and at ease. Of course, I followed. I guess I was scared because all I remember is looking down at each step I took. Looking down at my new pretty red shoes. Probably beaming with pride that I could walk in a circle and not fall (an accomplishment I came to find out is really not such a big deal!). Trying so, so hard to be like my brother...walking with confidence; not falling. Somehow in my puny brain, the not falling... doing it right...took on gargantuan meaning.

Growing up in my family was not tragic, but it was challenging. My father was a confusing man; kind and loving at times, gruff and sarcastic at others. To look at him, one saw a boyish big guy with a mischievous smile and a wicked laugh (wicked in a good way). Dad was the second to youngest of ten children. I don't know much about his childhood other than that he was part of an intact family and was close to both his parents. My grandfather was a city laborer and worked long hard hours doing anything and everything he was told. He was tall and strong with a lovely boyish face. My grandmother was a devoted mother who gave love as she could and allowed her children to be who they were. Dad lived in a two-story home, where, if you saw it now, you could not imagine twelve people cohabitating without killing each other! I guess that's how most folks lived in the 1920's and 1930's. I remember seeing a picture of Dad when he was about eight or nine. He was dressed in his knickers and argyle socks, sitting in front of a fireplace with a large black pipe propped perfectly in his mouth. He was holding up what appeared to be a rocks glass filled with some liquid. Dad mimicked that picture in real life for years to come, as you soon will see.

Dad served in Korea for two tours of duty. The second being a pivotal one. He spoke little about his experiences there, but did say it wasn't really "his thing." Dad was a soft-spoken gentle man, but as an Air Force Staff Sergeant, he had to be a tough bastard; whether he wanted to or not. I think that was conflicting for him. He was the guy doing, not the guy telling and screaming to do. It just wasn't his nature. Looking back, his military service played havoc with his emotions. Dad was not the best with sharing emotion, or letting anyone in for that matter; at least not before I turned twelve. He was the man of the house, and his job was to make money and support his family. Outward love and tenderness fell by the wayside. Now don't get this wrong...Dad would say he loved me (when I said it first) and hugged me and kissed me (when I did it first). I just wish it could have been more spontaneous on his end.

Dad was a nervous man. My earliest memories are of him smelling like a combination of smoke and whiskey. Dad liked to go out to the VFW, Elks Lodge, and any other lodge to kick back. Maybe he needed that escape to forget he was a husband and dad and forget all the responsibilities he shouldered, if only for a little while. Dad's frequent choice to be absent caused friction between him and Mom (we'll get to Mom shortly). She would often pick up the rotary phone in the kitchen and dial the VFW and tell him to come home. Do you know I KNEW each time she called him by the number of clicks the phone made? I learned that super early as if to plan my escape for when the yelling started. You can't blame Mom for wanting Dad home. For that matter, you can't blame Dad for going. This word "blame" will be discussed at length later in the book.

Dad was a draftsman by trade and a skilled carpenter. He built custom cabinets which are in my family's house to this day. He built an addition to our very small Cape Cod home and created an extra room in the basement. Dad was super talented. Looking back, I wonder if he saw that in himself...even a little bit. I remember the family room "going up" with the structural beams and make-shift steps. As a kid I was completely dumbfounded. How on earth could this become a room? A REAL room. I remember watching him work with his big burly tool belt around his waist, a cigarette clenched in his lips, and an ice cold Budweiser usually close by. That was Dad: Simple, precise, determined.

Dad was also active with my brother in sports. He coached my brother's little league teams and guided my brother with his football skills. I remember one time at a Little League baseball game, the umpire made a rotten call. "A shitty call," remembering Dad's vernacular. Anyway, Dad finished the game in the dugout, but then made a beeline for the umpire as he tried to leave the field. Dad was on fire. I had never seen him so upset and so ready for a fight. "C'mon, c'mon...you want to start something?" I remember Dad saying. This was not good, my sister and I kept asking Dad to leave. Dad switched from his rage at the umpire to a soft calming voice...saying to my sister and I, "It's okay, don't worry...go find your mother." Looking back, as I write this, that was very cool of him. In the heat of this potential slam down, Dad caressed our emotions. Maybe he was not so closed off after all. Dad left the parking lot, no punches thrown, no profanity flung. Phew! Luckily, there were no other altercations with league officials after that. I never asked Dad what fired him up so much that day. Maybe my brother was slighted (or Dad thought so). Maybe it was a trigger from his own childhood. Who really knows? I will forever remember Dad choosing not to make that day into a shit show.

Dad's smoking and drinking, although very typical for that time, would eventually be his downfall (remember that photo of him with the pipe and the glass in hand?). I guess that was his comfort zone. He contracted rheumatic fever as a child which weakened his heart. That combined with his adult lifestyle was a perfect storm for significant heart disease later on. He was not an alcoholic or excessive smoker (at least I don't think so). He was anxious; nervous. He used these substances to feel calm. Perhaps regain control. Who could blame him? There is that word blame again which I will address later.

My Mom was a tender, good person. She was a hugger. Her story is a dilly. Mom was born in 1933 within a year of her older sister's death. Grandmom's daughter Mary had died of the flu. Grandmom, from what I have come to understand, suffered from long-standing mental health issues. In this day and age, she would have probably been diagnosed with moderate depression or bipolar

DAD WAS A NERVOUS MAN. MY EARLIEST MEMORIES ARE OF HIM SMELLING LIKE A COMBINATION OF SMOKE AND WHISKEY.

disorder. Back then...unstable; crazy. Grandmom was known to have burned my Aunt Josie's homework (Aunt Josie being Mom's oldest sister) convinced it was the devil's propaganda. Considering Grandmom lost and gained a child within one year, she was probably all over the map. My mother was born in Perth Amboy hospital and shortly after returning home with her baby girl, Grandmom began exhibiting shocking, erratic behaviors. She became more aggressive towards my grandfather and her other children. She spoke in a confusing and rambling way. She was not well. My grandfather quickly decided to contact social services to protect his family, especially my infant mother. Mom was returned to the hospital for three months while the family sorted things out. They say the mother/ child bond is strongest within the first six months of life. Mom never had that. Looking back, that must have been awful. It was determined that Grandmom needed to be institutionalized for severe mental illness (something more commonly done then). Aunt Josie was asked by my grandfather to become a surrogate mother; not just to Mom, but to her four other siblings. She would have to quit school, learn how to take care of a newborn, and keep house. She was fifteen. Aunt Josie was a stellar student with an active teenage social life. She had plans. These were not them. I remember Mom telling the story of the social worker coming to their house explaining to Aunt Josie what she would have to do; to give up; to sacrifice. As my aunt pondered this monumental decision, she looked over and saw my grandfather crying in the corner of the room. She had to do it. As I write this now, I have such admiration and gratitude to Aunt Josie. I did not remotely understand as a child the unprecedented sacrifice she made. The family would have been split up and have been put in foster care or state institutions. She kept everyone together...and Mom never forgot her for that.

Mom grew up poor but was cared for. She would often say, "Everyone was poor, but we didn't know it." Her older siblings (especially my Aunt Reggie) took Mom everywhere and did what they could to help around the house and help raise Mom. Aunt Reggie, as the stories go, was a 'toughie'. She did not take crap from anyone. One day while walking home, Mom and Aunt Reggie were confronted by two teenage girls. "Just ignore them...keep walking," Mom recalled. The girls persisted until one pushed a major button. One girl evidently said,"Don't you live in that crazy house?" That was NOT a word Aunt Reggie took lightly considering Grandmom's mental health issues. It was then that Aunt Reggie (all 5 feet 2 and ten years of age) turned around, fists in the air and yelled, "Come

on...you want to fight...come on!!" Mom remembered being frozen and terrified. After what seemed to be hours, the girls reconsidered and ran off. Mom stared up at Aunt Reggie as if she were a God. Aunt Reggie just smiled and said, "No one will pick on us again...let's go home." Mom was five years old.

Even though Mom grew under the watchful and (sort of) tender affection from her siblings, she was still missing the tenderness of a mother. Aunt Josie tried hard, but she was a teenager who was internally angry and resentful that her life was yanked out from under her. Mom recalled wanting more hugs and kisses from Aunt Josie, but to no avail. Aunt Josie had work to do and no time for much else. Mom relied on her father for that physical comfort. And he delivered. He was affectionate and loving, smothering my mother with hugs and kisses. Mom liked that. Even though it was not from a mother, it was love. Grandpop would take Mom to the beach and to outdoor concerts. He would proudly show her off at local polka dances, and Mom would not disappoint. She learned how to polka (and polka well) by age three! Mom remembered Grandpop wanting her to polka dance one day, and Mom responded with, "If you buy me a hot dog, I'll dance." He bought her the hot dog and they danced. Mom would laugh in recalling that story saying, "What a little snot I was, huh Sue?" Not a little snot at all; just a clever child who got what she wanted.

Mom would speak occasionally about visiting Grandmom in the psychiatric hospital. She recalled how the staff would graciously have Grandmom dressed and sitting in the waiting room when they first walked in. Sometimes Grandmom would be present and alert, sometimes scattered and rambling. It was hell for Mom. Not only did she endure her mother's episodes, she endured the screams and unpredictable behaviors of the other patients. This was not a place for small children, but it was the only place Mom could spend time with her own mother. As I write this, I wipe away tears. Grandmom was institutionalized for almost twenty-five years before being sent to a rest home and then a care facility. She lived to be ninety-three years old, and Mom always included her for holiday dinners and family celebrations. She was still her Mom.

Mom and Grandpop had an extremely close bond; perhaps filling emotional voids of their partial lives. Then when Mom was ten years old, Grandpop became ill with a kidney infection. Nothing at all bad these days. Antibiotics and rest. But this was 1943. Grandpop contracted blood poisoning and died shortly afterward. Mom was devastated. This vibrant happy man who gave her so much love was gone. Mom recalled the wake being in their living room (as was common at the time). It was customary for someone to remain with the deceased 24/7 to ward off evil spirits. Mom was not "on the clock" exactly, but she did sneak into the living room at night. She told me about how she stared at her father wanting to cry, but feeling like she couldn't, or shouldn't. She did not completely understand what had happened, but she knew more changes were ahead.

Aunt Josie and the family moved several times in order to make ends meet. Mom's siblings were now all in their late teens and twenties, so they all pitched in to meet the family responsibilities. Mom said she was never hungry and never felt truly alone. That was a blessing. She did not like moving so much, but later in life she made peace with it. She understood later they were keeping the family together instead of splitting it apart. Eventually, Aunt Reggie got married, as did the other siblings. Aunt Josie remained single and continued to care for Mom. She did have a serious boyfriend, but he was tragically killed in World War II; another loss. Many years later, Aunt Josie married and quickly divorced. This later-in-life marriage was not a healthy one as her husband was emotionally abusive. Aunt Josie remained single for the rest of her life and remained active until her own mental health came into question. Mom took on her care and placed her in a safe and competent care facility. Mom often said she owed her that.

Mom and Dad met in high school and were married in 1962. They moved to a house in Fords, New Jersey which became my one and only childhood home. It was Dad, Mom, my older brother, and younger sister. Five people and one bathroom. But hey...it was 1968.

CHAPTER TWO

IN THE BEGINNING...SOME MORE

I knew at a young age I was kind of different. In watching old home movies, my face says it all: usually a quizzical bewildered look...as if to say, "What the F*ck?" I remember looking at books with words and pictures and focusing on the pictures. They told me the story. When I did look at the words, it was pure memorization, little comprehension. I realized that if I watched something closely, I would learn it. Maybe not understand every nuance of it, but I would learn it. Like when Mom was teaching my brother how to tie his shoes (a prerequisite for Kindergarten). She would go over and over it with him, as I sat right there following her every move. She would take the "big loop and put it through the hole and then tie it... yeah." That was Mom's mantra every single time. Wouldn't you know I learned how to tie my shoes long before my brother! Mom was proud and I felt good. Watching was my ticket anywhere.

I remember listening to conversations and usually being a half step behind with its meaning or punchline, and then laughing or saying something clever to hide the fact that I was not keeping up. Sometimes I did not have one clue what was being said...not one. I was not doing it "right." When my bewildered expression would overcome me, my brother and sister would laugh and call me names. I know that's typical sibling stuff, but they knew my weaknesses and at times preyed on them. I felt stupid and less then...and most importantly: alone. I liked any attention I got from Mom and Dad, so I did anything to please them. I liked the gold stars and the pictures on the refrigerator. Why didn't we have a bigger refrigerator? My self esteem could have used it! When my brother did start Kindergarten (and by the way, he learned how to tie his shoes!) it was just Mom and my sister and I at home. I liked that. Mom and I would cuddle and watch God knows how many children's shows. And every weekday, we would tune in to her soap opera, All My Children. She was a freak for that show! Again, I only learned through watching and repeating in my head over and over and over. That was exhausting by the way. I realized young that I needed to repeat words and visions many times over to "get it." Was everyone like this? I had no idea. I just knew I was.

When my brother would come home from school, he would talk about what he did and the friends he had. As much as I liked my time with Mom, I was intrigued by this school thing. Sounds good, I thought. He would bring home papers and Mom would go gaga over them and hang them up...on the refrigerator! Wow...more pictures on the refrigerator! Only this time they were from SCHOOL! Since I had no way of knowing my learning style was unique (or I guess, delayed) I had no apprehensions about my own first day of Kindergarten. That day is crystal clear in my mind. Thirty-seven kids, (got the exact number from the school records) half of whom were screaming for their mothers. I made a beeline for my assigned chair, and put my head on the desk. I distinctly remember saying to myself, "Don't cry!" And I didn't. At the end of that first day, Mom was waiting outside in the parking lot with the other anxious moms. I remember that classroom door flying open and running outside into my mother's arm. She picked me up and swung me around from side to side. I loved that! She was smiling down at me and I up at her.

I quickly discovered what I was good at in Kindergarten; not printing or drawing...roll call. Every day was roll call. The same time, the same way, every day. The teacher would open this heavy loose-leaf binder which contained individual student information sheets. One by one, she would recite a student's name while flipping the page. And we all knew the expected and anticipated response: "Here." One day I distinctly remember chiming in with her as she read the names aloud. I was looking down at my desk, and my mouth was moving in perfect synchronicity with hers. It was loud enough for her to hear, because after getting through at least ten or so, she stopped. I kept going. The class started to laugh and I froze. I mean froze! This was Catholic School. You did not do ANYTHING without being instructed to do so. Oh man, that was it. Back to watching All My Children full-time until I died of old age! After what felt like a lifetime, I looked up and saw the teacher staring and smiling at me. Okay... good sign, I thought. Very quietly she said, "Miss Bisaha, would you come here please?" Still okay, I thought. As I stood next to her, I remember her closing the book completely then opening it from the beginning. She did not say a word. She just pointed to the first name on the first page and let me have at it. Each page she

I HAD TO KEEP BEING INNOVATIVE. I SO WANTED TO BE LIKE MY BROTHER AND SISTER.

flipped I uttered the student's name. Did not miss one out of thirty seven students! I remember when she got to the end, I looked up and the class was silent and staring at me. Dumbfounded. The teacher said, "very good Susan" and began to clap. So did the class. I liked that.

As happy and proud as I was with my roll call conquest, I quickly realized not all learning was that simple. I remember making these paper plate clocks in first grade. We each took a paper plate and fastened the cut-out clock hands in the center. That part I could do. It was the concept of telling time that befuddled me. For some reason, I could not get the concept of the hands telling me what time it was (don't worry, folks, I'm all good with it now!). Weird how I could memorize and spit out thirty seven names, but could not tell you it was 3:30 on a clock! Again, I figured out how to get by. My quick wit and excellent hearing allowed me to act like I had the answer. Along with asking the person in front of me for the answer! Cheating...maybe. Survival... definitely! My brother and sister grasped that concept a lot quicker and they made sure to let me know it. Again, I felt stupid and alone. But again, I knew I had ways to get through. I had to keep being innovative. I so wanted to be like my brother and sister. They were cool and on top of things. They knew all the latest jokes and their meanings. They had lots of friends. Me...not. I never remember Mom or Dad making fun of me or criticizing. I just remember thinking...no...knowing...I didn't want to make any mistakes. I wanted everyone to be proud of me. I wanted to be special.

Throughout grammar school, I had a couple of friends, but I certainly was not popular. One friend in particular was Tommy. Tommy was quiet and smart and cute and funny. He became my best friend all though grade school. We did homework together, belonged to the same clubs in school and played at each other's houses. He was my bud. Interestingly, I saw him mostly as a friend, not a boyfriend. I think he thought the same about me. Never ever did we experiment with kissing or even holding hands. Our destiny was a platonic one. Looking back, Tommy helped me weather lots of storms. And he helped me with my schoolwork. Such a pure soul; at least back then.

Charm and fast thinking became my survival skills throughout elementary school; along with volunteering for EVERYTHING. I learned early that you did not need intelligence for eagerness, and man was I eager. I learned that a walk to the Main School office could get me out of answering questions and feeling stupid. Of course while there, I would

offer to help unpack textbooks, run errands for the school secretary, deliver toilet paper to the bathrooms. Whatever, man...I was so there! I especially loved Christmas Fundraising season. Each student was expected to take a cardboard box filled with cards, gift wrap and assorted gifts and...well...sell them to anyone and everyone. Of course all these cardboard boxes had to be sorted and labeled and delivered. And OF COURSE, I was there. Susan became the frequent flyer; and just like Fed Ex, I always delivered. But let's face it; I could not live in the Main Office. Eventually, I had to go back to class.

Insatiable eagerness combined with razor sharp body language interpretation was my ticket. I continued to use clever tactics to avoid the ever-growing fear that people would realize I was slow. Man, did I learn how to be charming; not deceitful or manipulative, just sweet and charming. I learned how to maneuver out of not knowing an answer or when I could not formulate a word. I did everything from fake an incessant sneezing attack, to intentionally break a pen in my hand to go to the restroom, to compliment the teacher for...well...anything! Nothing lasts forever, so of course there were times when I did have to answer a question I did not know. It was excruciating. My stomach would get tight and I would have trouble breathing. The entire class would become either silent or start laughing. Imagine your mouth wants to give an answer but your brain does not tell you what the answer is. To this day, I cannot tell you what my learning issue is. Perceptual impairment, delayed reading comprehension; who knows. And, to this day, it still happens. I still freeze and occasionally cannot form words. And still I use humor and charm to cover up interpreted stupidity. And to this day I am a master at body language. It blows my clients away. But that's for later.

I was in near complete control of things up until eighth grade. Until then, I was able to handle challenges and to get out of practically anything. All was good. You know what they say about life. Life is what happens while you are busy making other plans.

CHAPTER THREE

LET THE CHILDREN COME TO ME...

The summer before eighth grade was filled with change, excitement and fear. The change came when my older brother told me that kids were needed to work in the Church rectory. The "work" meant answering phone calls, writing out Mass cards, answering the door, and giving out keys to Church organizations for meetings and get-togethers. My friend Tommy wanted to work there too, so it was absolutely perfect. I could make some money, have some independence, and spend more time with my best friend. Most importantly, all this meant getting out of the house. Mom and Dad were arguing more. They seemed to be drifting apart. Dad became the VFW Commander (which had a bar) and was out of the house even more than before. His occasional "out for a beer" nights turned into daily occurrences. Looking back, it must have been very hard for Mom to take care of us, the house, and a husband who seemed to value "the guys" more than his wife and kids. I know now that was not the case, but back then...what else could it be? Mom was not pleased. Those telephone calls to Dad from the rotary phone (the one I memorized the clicks on) were increasing. And each phone call was met with more and more anger. I remember going outside A LOT; shooting baskets anywhere I could, hitting tennis balls for hours by the Siperstein's paint store. I needed more 'out time'. and working at the rectory was the blissful solution.

For those of you who are not Catholic, a rectory is the place where the parish priests and visiting priests live. It's like any other house; it has bedrooms, a living room, a kitchen, a laundry room. We were the "rectory rats"...young kids paid a dollar an hour to do whatever Father Whoever told us. Sounds boring. Trust me...nothing was further from the truth. Remember...these were the same men who stood in the pulpit week after week spewing the word of God and preaching what to do and what not to do. In other words, they were a millimeter below God himself. They did no wrong. I remember writing down everything my brother told me about how to answer the phones and how to greet visitors. I would study those notes and took pictures in my head of what was where. I wanted to be good at this. And I did NOT want to make any mistakes.

That summer I made some money and felt grown up and responsible. It was good.

The excitement arrived when, at the beginning of eighth grade, one of the rectory priests, Father Marcus, visited our classroom (I vaguely remember him moving into the rectory towards the end of that summer). He had a presence about him. His black suit was perfectly starched, his cologne wafting through the doorway...and the entire classroom. He was not very tall, but he carried himself with great confidence. His smile was charming and he had a booming voice. He was someone that drew you in. So Marcus introduces himself and immediately began passing out papers. He explained these were papers to join the CYO (Catholic Youth Organization) I distinctly remember him saying (not asking) that we were to sign the paper before he left. He told us the Catholic Youth Organization was "the cool thing." We would go on all sorts of trips, volunteer for local charities, have dances, and conduct fundraisers. We got to have fun and be free. And we all HAD to join. To be honest, I did not think to hesitate to join for one second. Why? Simple. All these cool things translated in my head to one small phrase, 'OUT OF THE HOUSE'. If I thought working at rectory afforded me time away from my increasingly unhappy household, this was indeed the golden ticket. "Thank you God!" I distinctly remember saying in my head. You must really love me to bring me this great priest, and this great group.

I remember one day working at the rectory when Marcus came into the work room. In making small talk he recalled me as one of the eighth grade students on sign-up day. He asked how things were going and how I liked working there. "It's really good," I remember saying. I wanted him to like me. He talked about some upcoming fall events with the CYO and how he hoped to see me at every one of them. When he left the room, his cologne lingered for hours (kind of like when he was in the classroom). I felt something good, but very different. I was only thirteen at the time and had no real frame of reference with life and its many possibilities. From that day on, he made sure to see me on the days I worked at the rectory. He would ask me about my family and friends, school, etc. He seemed to really care.

I soon began to notice the plethora of people Marcus would bring through the rectory and upstairs to his private room. Or as it was later called "the inner sanctum." There were older people, mostly male, and younger people...all male. I came to understand they were acquaintances of his in his former churches. Since I worked at the rectory afternoons, evenings and

weekends, I began to see, hear and smell some interesting stuff. I saw several boys around my age; maybe a tad older. I heard raucous laughter and dicey verbiage as they would enter the rectory through the garage. And I would smell a combination of sweet smoke and liquor (growing up with my father and considering my quick attention to detail, you could not get much past me). I remember initially thinking this is not the way it "should" be. A priest "should not" be fraternizing with this many people, especially this many young people. Then again, I had nothing to compare it to. This was the only rectory I had ever worked in. Maybe this happened everywhere and I was a sinner for thinking ill of him, and of them. Yep, I was a sinner and needed to stop my judgmental thoughts and accept. When I would go into the rectory kitchen, I could hear the goings-on pretty clearly. Marcus' room was directly above the kitchen. I heard the laughing and music. God, it sounded like such fun. Then the intercom would buzz with the ever predictable request, "A bowl of ice please." That meant filling a glass bowl to the brim with ice and walking it upstairs to his private room. I lived for those days! I got to see up close and personal the "inner sanctum" filled with the chosen ones. The ones he wanted to be with. God almighty I wanted that to be me. Week after week, I would work more and more hours, jumping at the chance to cover someone's time slot. And when I did, I was not disappointed.

GRADUALLY, HE BEGAN SPENDING MORE TIME IN THE RECTORY WORKROOM TALKING AND ASKING ME ABOUT DAD. HE WOULD GIVE ME HUGS AFTER OUR TALKS; INNOCENT AT FIRST, LIKE A FATHER TO A CHILD.

At some point, Marcus told me that the Monsignor (the boss in the rectory) was having trouble sleeping. To assist with this, Marcus would make him "special coffee"...otherwise known as black coffee with whiskey...no milk, no sugar. He showed me once how to make it, "Exactly as Monsignor liked it." And very soon, in addition to commands for bowls of ice, Marcus would require, "Monsignor's special coffee." That meant move fast! That meant brew up that coffee quickly and fill the coffee cup at least halfway with Irish whiskey. Bring it upstairs with the ice, and then dutifully return to the workroom. Like clockwork, I would deliver the goods, come downstairs, then hear Marcus's door open and his footsteps move down the hallway. I would hear another door open, a muffled exchange of words, and finally footsteps back to the "inner sanctum." Marcus was the dutiful son in a way, delivering Monsignor's elixir to rest easy. I felt like I was part of some covert operation. The adrenaline would rush through me on my delivery days. Looking back, I felt he trusted me with these monumentally important tasks and I was not about to disappoint. At least not until my lapse of judgment one particular day. I remember feeling super tired and nodding off in the waiting room. It was a Saturday afternoon. Somewhere around two or three o'clock, Marcus summoned for Monsignor's "special coffee." I made it as usual, only this time I added milk. I distinctly remember Marcus's face when I handed him the cup. He rolled his eyes and gave me this wicked stare I had not seen from him up to that point. I remember him saying, "You DON'T put milk in Monsignor's special coffee." And with that he hurriedly walked past me down the stairs to prepare another cup. I heard the coffee cup loudly crashing in the sink, and him blowing out air the whole time, like a child who isn't happy they have to go to bed. He was mad, and I was devastated. How could I be so stupid! How could I make such a mistake! How could I let this happen! My whole world seemed to crumble. No, really, I mean it! I had come to really like Marcus and the life he lived. I really REALLY wanted to be part of that life. And now... well...forget it! My fuck-up was forever. I remember writing Marcus a ridiculously long apology letter and putting it on his desk in his office. I have no idea if he ever read it, but for weeks I begged God that he would.

Finally in late fall, early winter of my eighth grade year, the fear took over. Dad had gone to the doctor which was rare for him...I do not remember that being part of his normal routine. One thing led to another; he was put in the hospital, and within a week, he was diagnosed with Congestive Heart Failure and/or cardiomyopathy. The rheumatic fever he had suffered as a child paired with his drinking and smoking was that perfect storm leading to heart disease. And this was a bad, bad heart disease to have. Dad was only fifty years old, but this was the early 1980's. Cardiomyopathy was nowhere near where it is today with treatments and options. The treatments were lots and lots of medicines. The options (well, one option, really) was a heart transplant. Again, nowhere near what it is today. Dad kept the transplant option a secret from all of us. We did not know that that was even on the table until years later. Our lives became a whirlwind of unknowns. At first, Dad just slept a lot. He had to retire early under disability retirement. Physically, he did whatever he could (which was not much most days).

As if Mom and Dad's relation- ship was not strained enough, this was the icing on the cake. Mom was working full-time and became two parents for the three of us. She was it.

I remember those weeks and months watching Dad sleep, hearing these wretched loud breaths come from his mouth; his garbled congested coughs increasingly frequent. I hated it. I remember one day him lying in his bedroom. When he heard me walk by, he asked me to come in. "Hey, Sue, can you listen to my chest," he said. I nervously complied and pressed my ear against his chest. I heard low, garbled sounds, and although I wasn't a doctor, I knew it didn't sound good. When he asked what I heard, I simply said, "Nothing Dad, you sound great!" He smiled and closed his eyes to nap. I wanted so so much to be there for him, but I was scared out of my mind. Mom did not talk much of Dad's illness, never mind his prognosis. I threw myself into CYO activities. I think I went to every general meeting, every committee meeting and every event sponsored. I was exhausted, but at least I was out of the house. I also took more hours working at the rectory. Sometimes on the weekends, I would work from 8 am to 10 pm straight. I would try to call friends, but using the rectory phone was off limits, and somehow Monsignor knew when you were on personal calls. In my solitude there, I began confiding in Marcus. Sometimes, he would wander in and sit on the couch and talk. Sometimes I would go into his office and talk. He seemed very interested in Dad's illness and very compassionate with my plight. He would pray with me and encourage me to pray every chance I got. Prayer was the key to every situation. He told me that morning mass was a great time to pray, and since he was the celebrant on most mornings, it gave me a chance to see him more. And I did want to see him more. Thus began a morning routine of attending 6:30 am Mass, then a quick trip to the donut shop (or as we later called it "Our Lady of Dunkin Donuts") and then school. Most days after school was working at the rectory or basketball practice, so anyway you sliced it, I was never home.

Since our neighbor was usually up and out early each morning, he would often offer me a ride to morning mass. My mother said I could not go unless I had a ride, so that was that. To be honest, sometimes I did walk the three quarters of a mile myself in the dark. Not smart looking back, but nothing was going to stop me. The neighbor would motion for me to come into his car as I would walk past his house. It was an old car with an old smell, and he was an old man. It started with him putting his hand on my leg as he drove. That progressed to his hand in between my legs. When we finally arrived at church (a five-minute drive which seemed like an hour), he would stop the car and pull me close to him sticking his tongue in my mouth. It was wet and gross. And I was scared and alone. After the first time, I thought that was it. No more. Time after time, it happened over and over with money beginning to be exchanged. "Go buy some candy after school," he would say. Sometimes, I would run past his house in the pitch black of mornings praying he would not see me. Sometimes he saw me and drove up behind me yelling to get in the car. And each time I did. Crazy? No. Desperate? Not desperate. I needed to be out of my house. Out of ear shot of Dad's coughing, and bumping into things at night when he could not sleep. And if this is what I had to exchange for being away from Dad, so be it. An acceptable loss according to military jargon. Back then, there was little to no education on inappropriate touching. And it really wasn't so bad. I convinced myself of that.

After each morning Mass, I would meet Marcus in the sacristy (that's offstage from the altar). Sometimes he would go with me to Our Lady of Dunkin Donuts. And there were times Marcus would scoot out the door as soon as Mass was over, not waiting for my morning hello. Those hurt. One day, I told him about the neighbor. He listened and seemed concerned. He told me he himself would pick me up some mornings or he would send a CYO advisor (an adult volunteer) to pick me up. He said how great it was that a young person like me would get up so early and so often to attend Mass. He said he liked people like that. "Hmmm," I thought. "Am I getting closer to being one of his chosen?" Am I approaching an invite to the inner sanctum?" Gradually, he began spending more time in the rectory workroom talking and asking me about Dad. He would give me hugs after our talks; innocent at first, like a father to a child.

One particular morning things were bad at home. In the middle of the night, Dad got very sick and needed to be taken out by ambulance to the hospital. I remember waking up to voices and noises in the living room combined with the clanging of metal and furniture. As I looked down the stairs, I saw my father being taken out on a stretcher with some kind of machine on top of him. I remember my brother coming halfway up the stairs saying, "Everything's going to be okay, but it wouldn't hurt to say a prayer right now." My brother and my mother left for the hospital as my uncle arrived to sit with me and my sister. I remember my uncle saying, "Go back to bed...I'll let you know what happens." Um....seriously? How

could we possibly go to sleep without knowing if Dad would live or die? The next few hours were excruciating. Shortly after daybreak, the phone rang with Mom saying Dad was in ICU. No other details other than that it was touch and go. I don't remember much after that, but I can tell you Dad pulled through. He pulled through many more hospital stays over the next several years. More of that to follow.

Needless to say, I needed Marcus to comfort me. His words and prayers were always soothing, as if God himself had his arm around me. When I saw Marcus the next day at the rectory, I was distraught; sobbing uncontrollably. I went into the bathroom to get a tissue and he followed me. He stood behind me and put his hands on my shoulders. Then he reached over and shut the bathroom door and shut off the light. I could see his reflection in the bathroom mirror; he had a smirk on his face. In a matter of seconds, he turned me to face him and pressed his body into mine. His hands were rubbing my back and he was repeatedly saying, "You are such a good girl...you are such a good friend." This kind of affection was new for him and me. But honestly, it felt good. I felt close to someone who loved me. He was comforting me. Then to my surprise, he reached behind me and untucked my shirt from my pants. He lifted the shirt just over my hips so that it was hanging out. He then began caressing my buttocks over the pants. Squeezing, rubbing...all the while saying, "You are such a good girl." Looking back I am horrified by his actions. I'd just told him my father could be at death's door (not to mention him knowing of the neighbor's actions) and this is what he does! At the time, though, he said I was a good girl...and I believed every word. We stayed in the bathroom for several more minutes until he turned the light back on and opened the door. Then he left down the hall and went upstairs to his "inner sanctum." No words, no explanations. I was left in that room alone, not knowing what the heck had just happened; but one thing was crystal clear: I was now as special as the countless young people he spent time with. I was a member of the "inner sanctum."

From then on, there were dozens of encounters in bathrooms, the kitchen, the laundry room, and his office...all following the same pattern. He would call me in, shut the door behind me, shut off the lights and pull me close. He would caress my buttocks and slowly glide his hand down. The days of caresses over the pants were over. He graduated to slipping his hand under my pants and underpants. Firmly squeezing my buttocks to the point of pain at times. He would simultaneously pull me

closer and closer to him, and often I could feel his erect penis through his pants. Moaning, breathing hard, his patter was the same, "You are such a good girl...you are such a good friend." At times, he would suddenly stop and listen for people outside of where we were. He would motion for me to be quiet, and he would make faces at the door, like sticking out his tongue or fake laughing as if to say to whomever was out there, "Nah, nah...you can't catch me." It was one big game; the Marcus game of let's see how much I can get away with! Sick. These became our rituals. I was convinced I really WAS his special friend and could do no wrong in his eyes. Nope, not true. Remember the coffee incident? The colossal fuck-up that took place months before? I can assure you that did not happen again, but something else did.

One day, Marcus called me into his office and handed me the phone. I was on hold with someone, and I was instructed to wait as long as I had to, until an actual person came on. I was to IMMEDIATELY tell Marcus when that occurred. I remember being on that phone for close to an hour. I watched the clock. I watched him walking in and out of the office doing other things. I was getting tired, but God damn it, I was going to do it right and make him happy. I could tell he was getting more and more agitated at "them" (whoever "them" was). When an actual person finally came to the phone and said, "Hello, may I help you?" It was my time to shine. I had rehearsed my exact script to impress, "Yes, my name is Susan and I am holding for Father Marcus, please hold on." That turned out to be a very bad move. My wordiness was just enough for the person at the other end to hang up...as if to say, "I don't give a rat's ass who you are, I am busy!" I remember Marcus grabbing the phone from me with the same look of disdain he had with the coffee screw-up. The line was quiet and I was devastated. You would think I shot someone right then and there or mugged a senior citizen. HE WAS PISSED! My heart was pounding... I mean, out of my chest. I remember my one hand shaking. Marcus slammed the phone down with the force of a title fighter and then proceeded to lecture me on how stupid my actions were. How inconvenienced he now was because I messed up like that. And all the while, I sat there and took it. I was thirteen. I did my best. And now...strike two. I again fucked up royally. I remember him telling me to leave and the door slamming behind me. I went back to the workroom and cried and cried. How could I be so stupid?

Just like with the coffee debacle, I got back into Marcus' good graces.

In between his cold shoulder and temper tantrums, there were many strange yet humorous encounters. Father G. was another priest in the rectory at the time. A short large man...very large. And very loud. He would say Mass without a microphone and everyone could hear him. Whenever he had the 6:30 am mass, he would come onto the altar with his hair mussed and face unshaven. Guess he was not a morning person. He also had the record for the quickest morning Mass on record...less than ten minutes. For you non-Catholics, trust me...that is quite a feat! He talked so fast and gave out communion like he was throwing a Frisbee. He was a character. After Father G. would say mass, he would often bolt out of church and leave in his car. The rumor/possibility/probability was that he was visiting a "cousin." His female cousin. That is what we were told. We thought we were terrible Catholics and sinners for even "thinking" Father had a mistress on the side. Well, that's pretty much what we were programmed to believe about ourselves. WE were the bad ones, not them. WE needed to repent, not them. Father G. was a good man, but like so many I met in my early years, a little misguided and sad.

Marcus and Father G. acted like little boys. When in the workroom at the rectory, they would often make these weird growling noises in the hallway, then come into the room and wrestle us to the ground. Father G. was quite strong, so when he held me down, I was not going anywhere! Then they pretended to beat me up. I know this must sound bizarre and unbelievable, especially being priests, but it really happened. Almost as if all their pent up feelings were released with abandon with a little horseplay. Marcus always took Father G's lead; like Robin to Batman. For the most part it was harmless and playful, but Father G. had a strong grip. Sometimes he would hold my wrists so tight I thought they would break. And when they would get on top of me, it felt even worse. There was nothing overtly sexual (at least I don't think so). I think they both enjoyed the dominance of the "game. "As quickly as they swooped in, they would leave, back to their jobs of being priests. Often I would go home and my wrists and back were sore and bruised. I never said a word. Weird for a thirteen year old to experience such things.

Working at the rectory on Sundays was an education in church business. The counting room was down the hall, and twice during each mass, an usher (always a man) would bring bags and bags of money into the rectory, past the work room and into the counting room. There were probably half a dozen volunteers in there counting dollars and coins.

I never saw so much money! One volunteer who was ALWAYS there

EVERY Sunday was Roy. A tall thin man, Roy always....and I mean ALWAYS had a cigarette hanging from him mouth. His big belly was a prominent trait. I liked Roy...at first. He reminded me of my Dad.... boyish face with the scent of a hard working guy. I was told at some point that Roy was in immediate need of an annulment. He had been married and wanted to remarry in the Catholic Church. Although he was already divorced from his first wife, an annulment was the only way. Annulments cost money...a good amount of money, not to mention they took time. Paper work and waiting could take years. So Roy worked out a deal with Marcus where Roy would trade painting and carpentry services in Marcus' private room for expediting the annulment. The work began. I remember seeing Roy the next week wearing painter's clothes and lugging supplies upstairs. I remember being summoned several times to run up tape measures, paint brushes, beverages, etc. That was when I saw Marcus' "inner sanctum" up close. Wow...I really made it now. How much more special am I? A small living room, narrow hallway, bathroom and back bedroom. Most people have these, and it was really nothing worth getting excited over. But it was his! I remember peeking in his bathroom and seeing his shelf filled with colognes. I was in the place where the rowdy gatherings took place, and I was sure I would be invited to one soon! One day when Marcus was out, Roy asked me to come upstairs and help him. When I walked into Marcus' living area, he asked if I would get up on a ladder and reach some spots that needed painting. I remember looking up and being confused because nothing needed painting, but I did what I was asked. As I stood on the ladder, he kept telling me to go higher with the paintbrush pointing to areas of the ceiling. I remember standing on my tip toes and reaching as high as I could. It was then that his one hand found its way to my buttocks and the other to the front of my genital area. "I'm making sure you don't fall," he said. I froze. I stood on that ladder and dabbed that paintbrush as fast as I could so that I could come down the ladder, when I started to walk down, he kept making up reasons for me to stay up there. I felt like I was in a trance. This was not really happening in a priest's room, especially in Marcus' room. But it was. He told me to go up and down the ladder at least three or four times. And each time, he held me exactly the same way. So by the time I was almost fourteen I was sexually violated by three different men. And each time, I never told a soul. Again, this was the early 1980's; most everything was different then. And even if I did tell, who would believe me? Besides, none of it was that bad. In a

crazy way, I thought I was special to Roy, too.

CYO activities continued, and by the spring, I had gotten to know John, one of the adult advisors. John was a quiet soft spoken man in his mid-thirties with two daughters a couple of years younger than me. He was divorced and enjoyed his Church involvement. He was a really nice guy. I don't know why, but we started spending time together. I would go to his apartment and watch movies with him and his daughters. We would take walks in the park. It was a different kind of special for me. We held hands and kissed once. That was it. Looking back, I know it was inappropriate on his part to forge this type of relationship with me, a thirteen year old. From my point of view, it was actually healthy. It was not as sexually driven as the other encounters, and he had kids. Ok, so he was almost twenty years older than me."So what," I thought. No real harm here. This went on until early high school which I will get into later.

That spring was also my first taste of a Battle of the Bands. It was a CYO-sponsored event held a few times a year to raise money for...well... never quite sure where the money went...but it raised money. Local bands would pay a fee to play their music and be judged (by Marcus and his inner sanctum friends). When I was asked to work security, I was again thrilled. He handpicked me! Not having a clue what security at a Battle of the Bands meant, I showed up super early that night and got ready for whatever. I would NOT disappoint Marcus again, not like the coffee and telephone incidents. The building was dark and loud and it got smokier as the night went on. It smelled like a pool hall. I was instructed to walk around, keep an eye out for drunken kids, and be on door duty. No one was allowed to reenter if they left the building. The walking around and door duty were a piece of cake. Helping out with the drunks? Are you serious? I was thirteen! But, as always, I did what I was told. Especially when Marcus pulled me into the kitchen where an obviously intoxicated teenager was leaning against the wall. He told me, "Stand here, hold her and DO NOT let her fall." As he was leaving I could hear him say, "If she falls, she could die." So here I am, standing with this semi-comatose girl praying she would just throw up and be okay. I remember my arms throbbing with pain as I braced her against the wall. She was mumbling and wanted to leave. I told her no. Just then, her knees buckled and she slid down to the floor. She literally fell to the floor like a collapsed building almost smacking her head on the cement. My heart stopped. My breathing stopped. I quickly snatched her up and put her back exactly as she was...standing against the wall. No good. Of course,

Marcus came in right then and saw my screw up. Strike three. "I TOLD YOU TO KEEP HER UP!" he bellowed. He pushed me out of the way, grabbed the girl rather forcefully and carted her out of the room. I did not see her again all night. Looking back I think Marcus was drunk too. As he pushed me aside, I got a clear and eye-tearing whiff of whiskey. No way around it. How could anyone put a thirteen year old in charge of an inebriated person? And then be pissed at me when he himself was inebriated? I'm telling you...it was A VERY different time.

As if that night wasn't bad enough, the final screw up came with the camera. John had asked me to hold his camera while he did security and door duty. I took the camera and put it in my bag in the kitchen. Never dreaming I would be pulled away to keep a drunken person alive, I thought it was safe. At the end of the night when John asked for his camera back, I reached in my bag realizing it was gone. I apologized profusely to John who at first was upset, but then mellowed and took it in stride. The next day John told Marcus about the incident, and Marcus agreed to pay for a new one. The agreement was I would pay back Marcus. At first I agreed (after all, it was my responsibility). But then I thought about it: these Battle of the Bands took in several hundreds of dollars. Refreshments another hundred or so. Coke and chips alone would have paid for another camera. But as punishment I had to pay. The same guy who by that time felt my bare butt dozens and dozens of times and got hard almost every time, made me pay. Since I did not have all the money right away, we agreed I would pay him in installments. Money wasn't exactly flowing to me at that time and I made no payments to Marcus for at least a few weeks. He approached me around that time to discuss. He stopped me in the rectory hallway and, with a scowl on his face said, "I CANNOT believe you haven't paid ANYTHING towards John's camera." Then he stomped up the stairs to his room. I heard his door open and slam shut. I tried to smooth things over by calling Marcus on the intercom asking if Monsignor wanted his special coffee. "NO!" Marcus shouted, and slammed down the phone. Confusing, humiliating, crazy.

Marcus kept his distance for a time after that. Like the girls on the playground who intentionally avoid the odd girl out. Paybacks? A well deserved lesson learned? Who knows? His behaviors were so erratic anyway; it was hard to know for sure. By now it was close to eighth grade graduation and two big things were happening. John and I were talking more and more. He would call at night. He and I would exchange mild

sexual banter. Nothing heavy, just playful. He told me how pretty I was and that if I was older, he would want to be with me. Keep in mind, I was thirteen and he was in his mid-thirties. The attention was addictive. I started babysitting his kids, spending more and more time with him and less time at the rectory. Nothing happened more than quick kisses and hand holding; almost as if he knew this was wrong so we would not make it "more wrong." When the rumors started flying about John and me, I noticed a big change in Marcus. He snapped out of his "I need distance from you" funk and became extra attentive. He was even more touchy-feely than before. He would ask for hugs several times a day. Was he actually jealous of John's affection? Was he a jilted lover plotting to get me back? Sure seems that way as I write this now. I will never know for sure, but I do know that Marcus prided himself on dominance and control. The stakes became greater.

The second big thing was our eighth grade class trip. Every year, the eighth grade class went to the Poconos for a full day of swimming, tennis, horseback riding and anything else young teens choose to do. The day ended with an evening dance, where we went from shorts and tee shirts to dresses and suits. Our teachers and a handful of parents were our chaperones, along with one distinctive priest; Marcus. We clambered up to the Poconos on a bus that I swore was built in the 1920's; loud and smelly. But, hey, it was taking us somewhere cool. We had all been given room assignments prior to leaving. Each room had four students and was our place to rest, shower, and watch TV, whatever. The adults also shared rooms. Except for Marcus. His was a private room. I remember sitting next to him on the bus ride up; making small talk and exchanging ideas of our plans for the day. Looking back, it really was like a boyfriend/girl- friend or husband/wife discussion, not kid to priest. He told me he wanted to see me throughout the day and I agreed. We arrived, and like typical kids tore through the wide open space and made a beeline for our rooms. Super cool. My first room without Mom and Dad. At least it was mine for that day. Marcus' room was close by and down a long hallway. I remember begging my mother for tennis clothes for the trip. Trust me, it was not to play tennis. At this point in my young life, I desperately wanted and needed to fit in. God love her, somehow Mom scraped money together and bought me a lovely matching shirt and shorts set. Not top of the line, but very pretty. I liked it. I hung out with my friends all day and did whatever they wanted. And Marcus was usually close by. Watching. Smiling. I liked that. At some point in the afternoon, Marcus said he wanted me to stop by his room. I remember thinking, "Ok, it's like the inner sanctum but in the Poconos...yes, yes!" We agreed on a time. Interestingly, as I write this now, I remember him repeatedly saying, "Don't let anyone see you. "As our time drew nearer I became more and more....well...not sure. Nervous? Excited? Worried? I say worried because several things had set him off in the past. Would there be another screw up that would leave him hating me again? Four strikes were on my record already, and that was enough. I remember leaving my friends in the game room and stopping off at my room to tidy up. My heart pounding and desperately trying to not be seen by others, I walked down the hallway to Marcus' room. The door was ajar slightly and I knocked quietly. I heard him say, "Susan? Come in." And I did.

So now we were in a different kind of room. This room was not a kitchen or laundry room or work room. This room was were people slept and took showers. His clothes were spewed on the bed and the TV was blaring loud. He was laughing and had this silly strange look on his face. I think he was drunk. No sooner did I close the door behind me than he had his hands all over me. He pushed me close to him with more force than other times. He immediately put his hand down the back of my tennis shorts and began touching and stroking. It happened so fast. His usual barrage of cologne overwhelmed my senses and I started to cough. He then let go. Without speaking, he took my hand and walked me over to the bed. He sat me down next to him and he again began the groping and touching. I started feeling weird, not excited. I wasn't sure if this was okay. I think he picked up on my discomfort, and offered me a drink. He got up and poured some whiskey or bourbon into two plastic cups. It was the middle of the afternoon on a Catholic school trip with adults everywhere. Did I take the drink...OF COURSE! That was the epitome of super cool. I remember sitting on the edge of the bed as he handed me this very strong concoction. Tasted a little gross, but I wasn't going to say boo. He sat next to me and we sipped our drinks. He and I were good again. After a few more swallows, he took the cup from my hand and put it on the nightstand. He then told me to lie on the bed on my stomach. I did. He began rubbing my back, then under my shirt. And as usual, he gravitated to my butt. After several minutes I felt him tug at my tennis shorts and moved them down below my hips. Suddenly I was completely exposed. That had never happened before. As God is my witness, he must have said, "You are such a good girl" a dozen times. As if to remind me that good girls do this. Out of nowhere, he suddenly stood up and said I

had to leave. I sheepishly pulled up my shorts, got off the bed and gave him one last hug. I remember him peering out of the curtains to make sure no one was near. I left feeling confused and numb. The whiskey or bourbon was kicking in and I needed to lie down (by myself). I went back to my room and rested for the next few hours. The next time I saw him was at our formal dance before heading home. He was in his perfectly pressed black suit, me in my pretty white dress. He did not come near me the rest of the night. On the bus ride home, he sat with one of the parents. Intentional? Maybe.

A few days later was graduation day. Since it was Catholic School, there was a mass along with the ceremony. I again wore my pretty white dress and I marched down that aisle proud as a peacock. There were several priests celebrating mass; Marcus being the head celebrant. Dad was feeling pretty good that day, so both Mom and Dad were there. I was so glad. Turns out during the awards portion of graduation, both Tommy and I received the "General Excellence" award. It was given to one boy and one girl from our eighth grade class. Don't ask me HOW on earth I got that award and WHY they picked ME. It made Mom and Dad so happy and proud. I was elated. Afterwards, my best friend Tommy and I had our picture taken together. I still have it. Remember him for later. And finally, the graduation party. As we had a large family with lots of aunts, uncles and cousins, Mom said I could only invite a few people. Marcus was one. My parents liked him as I told them how nice he was. They were thrilled to have "Father" at their home. Marcus sat in our backyard, wearing his perfectly pressed black suit, sipping a whiskey cocktail. Everyone knew he was our parish priest, and everyone liked him. Dad was enjoying the party. He and Marcus chatted about God, health and faith. Interesting.

CHAPTER FOUR

LOVE IS PATIENT...LOVE IS?????

High school. Some say it's the best time in your life. My first day of high school was actually the second day, having missed the first day due to an awful hangover. Of course, I told Mom and Dad I had a stomach virus and they fell for it...sorry folks! That was the beginning of many, many pseudo stomach viruses to come. And I immediately started behind the eight ball because I had not done a lick of my summer reading; resulting in six points taken off my Freshman English average. I really didn't care. Reading was far from my strong point and comprehension even worse. Believe it or not, somehow I did so well on the high school entrance exam that I was placed in all Honors courses! Seriously! What kind of angel or demon was sitting on my shoulder that test day? So on my second (which should have been my first) day of High School, I found myself in classes of eight to ten kids; total brainiacs. Okay. I was great at faking it. I was a master at being charming and witty. But this was a Herculean challenge here. What on earth could I pull out of my hat? AHA! Cheating! Now before you get all judgmental and wonder if my counselor's license is mail order or Photoshop, allow me to clarify. The majority of work I did in high school was in fact, my own. The C's and D's I got in some classes were my solo effort, baby! But I do admit to relying on some of the brainiacs for much needed assistance with shit I simply did not understand. I remember Cathy L; such a sweet, quiet, brilliant girl! She always, always gave me what I asked for. Looking back she really was an angel on earth. Was it right what I did? Of course not. Am I proud? No. Do I understand now why I did what I did? Absolutely. By the grace of God, freshman and sophomore years were fairly uneventful school-wise; I mostly pulled B's and C's with an occasional A.

I was still going to morning mass, but I convinced my parents that my friends from school were picking me up each morning. The truth was I got an occasional ride, but most times, I walked in the dark the three quarter mile distance. I was alone, but somehow never afraid. Must have been my Aunt Reggie's influence! My neighbor was not around as much (thank God) so that segment of my life dropped off.

Dad's health was erratic and unpredictable to say the least. When he was good, all was well. He would putter around the house fixing little things, run errands, and nap when tired. When he was bad, you just never knew. The day could start off "well" and I could leave the house in the morning with no worries, then come home to a note saying Dad's in the hospital...get here ASAP. And even when you got to the hospital, he could have been moved to a different room or floor. That was one of my most haunting memories; being given a room number from first floor reception, taking that five floor elevator ride with heart pounding and sweat accumulating, and finally arriving at said room to... someone who was not my Dad. Where the hell was my father? Anything was possible with his condition. One time I was told he was taken to the critical care wing because he had an "episode." Another time, he was out having tests. And one more time he was there in his assigned room, but tipped backward so that his head could get more blood flow. To a young kid, it was terrifying. Especially because I could often see the fear in his eyes. This strong handsome man was turning into a weak frightened shell. He could not be there for me or protect me anymore. He was drifting away.

The CYO was alive and well. In high school, we started going on re- treats. Fifty or so kids with a half dozen adults all camping out at an out- dated camp site and learning about God. There were late night prayer services, lectures on being a good Catholic, and talks on learning to love ourselves. Not to mention those who loved us while we were there. Marcus was in charge of the retreats. He would instruct the adult advisors to be with us during activities or in our cabins while he did God knows what. I remember being "summoned" on each retreat to come to Marcus' cabin (which of course was private) with sixty plus people within earshot. He would touch me, stroke me, and tell me what a good girl I was. One time, he had me sit on his lap and face him. He took my one leg and pulled it up over him near his shoulder. Kind of like a pair of scissors. I remember him laughing and pulling my leg up tight. It really, really hurt. Guess he didn't care. Then he held it there to have better access to my butt. He started this moaning thing where he would grunt and moan when I was close. Of

HE THEN BEGAN RUBBING MY BACK AND CARESSING MY LEG. I DISTINCTLY REMEMBER HIM SAYING "DON'T WORRY, I'LL MAKE IT ALL BETTER"

course the room was dark and of course he was hard. Looking back, I am amazed how arrogant he was to do this with so many people close by. The ultimate challenge of "the challenge." Besides, he was "Father;" who was going to doubt or question him? John was also on the early retreats. Now that took some juggling. Marcus feeling me up part of the time, John giving me emotional strokes at other times. All in one weekend! As I write this now, I cannot believe how many things happened with so many people around. And no one knew a thing. John was even more intense now that I was in high school, and seemed to kick it up a notch just like Marcus did in eighth grade. But John's behavior was more obvious and more people were starting to notice.

Sometime around the end of freshman year, the shit hit the major fan. I was still working at the rectory and Marcus called me upstairs to the inner sanctum. Cool, I thought. I could use an afternoon drink. Maybe there are others up there and we would party. When I got to his room the door was open. I knocked and entered. He was alone and looked troubled. He told me to come over to him and sit on his lap. I did. He then explained he knew all about John and was disgusted by his behavior. He said this was completely inappropriate and needed to stop. He said John had to be removed as an adult advisor. Wait...WHAT? How can this be happening? I began to shake and cry. He then began rubbing my back and caressing my leg. I distinctly remember him saying, "Don't worry; I'll make it all better." At that point, he said he had to call the other adult advisors for an emergency meeting. Since he said "he" had to call them, I started to get up off his lap. He wanted none of that. Without saying a word, he pulled me back onto his lap, held me tight with one hand and began dialing the phone with the other. He was calling Patty, one of the female adult advisors. As I sat there and listened and cried, Marcus said I had to talk to her and tell her it was all true. He handed me the phone and I told Patty everything. She told me to put Marcus back on the phone. They spoke briefly and Patty was on her way down. As soon as the phone receiver was placed back into the cradle, Marcus immediately slid his hand under my pants and underpants and began rubbing. The truth really is stranger than fiction! He held me close for a few minutes, and then he said he had other calls to make. He said I needed to leave. The switch yet again had flipped. He went from being so-called kind and caring to cold and distant. He evidently called the other adult advisors... as well as my parents.

When I got home later that day, I was met with angry and confused faces. Mom told me to sit with them in the kitchen. Mom explained she had gotten a phone call from Marcus and that we were all meeting with him the next morning. "Is there anything you want to tell us?" Dad asked. They told me to tell them everything. I remember starting to, but then being told to stop. "We don't need all the details," I remember Dad saying. Thank God! I did not WANT to give all the details! They said we would not speak of it again until the meeting the next day. Those several hours seemed like weeks on end. The next morning, I told my parents I would meet them at the rectory. When I got there, Marcus was in his office behind his desk. I sat in front of his desk on a leather chair, and waited. At first he was looking down doing paperwork, but then looked up at me and smiled and winked. He started making those weird noises he made when he was getting off; those grunting noises. He was laughing like this was all one big joke. Sick and twisted. A few minutes later, we heard the door open and one of the rectory rats let Mom and Dad in. I thought my heart was going to explode. I remember them entering Marcus' office and closing the door. My father shook Marcus's hand. I remember my parents staring at me, and the wrenching pain in my gut. Marcus proceeded to tell Mom and Dad that John was being removed from the CYO as per an emergency meeting with the other adult advisors. He told Mom and Dad how vile and unacceptable John's behavior was towards me and that this was NOT something he would allow in his organization. I distinctly remember him saying, "I will take care of this." I started to cry again and Mom and Dad just stared at me; no hugs of encouragement or compassion. That was hard. I guess they really did blame me for carrying on this "affair." Mom and Dad seemed to hang on every word Marcus said. They thanked him repeatedly for being so proactive. Mom even gave him a hug when the meeting ended!! Dad again shook his hand. I left the room while Mom and Dad stayed behind. Years later in my own therapy, I reflected back on that day with utter astonishment. My parents were in the very same office where Marcus repeatedly molested me. They sat on the same couch I sat on while being violated.

I remember coming home later that day and trying to talk to Mom. "It's taken care of," she said and went about her business. Looking back, I know she was angry at John, but it was sure projected onto me. That was hard. Thinking both your parents hate you for being a slut. After that day, I never saw John again.

My last clear memory of Marcus at that rectory was when he talked to me about confession. We were in the kitchen making something to

eat, and for some reason I remember asking him if he himself went to confession. "Oh yes," he said, quite proudly. He told me he confessed everything he did to his confessor (every priest had one...how convenient!) Now imagine...I was still trying to make sense out of everything that had happened, most recently; the meeting with Mom and Dad and feeling I was to blame. Marcus said he was bound to tell his confessor absolutely everything in his life. Then he said they would pray. All this while he is making a sandwich barely making eye contact.

Can you say WTF? I remember wondering if I should go to confession and spill my guts. Really spill them. Seemed like a quick fix; with a five-minute conversation, my soul would be saved. Cool. Even though I went to confession many times after that, I never spoke of Marcus or John. I figured they would blame me too.

CHAPTER FIVE

LOVE IS STILL PATIENT...BUT IT IS NOT KIND...

Sometime during my sophomore year, Marcus was transferred to another parish. I was devastated. No more rectory visits, no more feeling special. John was gone, and now Marcus was gone too. But his new church was very close to my High School. If I took the public transit bus, I could visit him, and visit I did. This was a Cathedral which meant the Bishop lived in the rectory. For you non-Catholics, a Bishop is like a Superintendent of Schools or regional manager of a Fortune 500 company. He was a big deal. I studied the public bus schedule, and Marcus began lining up dates to visit. I would show up at the Cathedral at about 3:00 in the afternoon in my Catholic school uniform and I would always meet him in the church sacristy (the backstage of the church altar). That was important; we ALWAYS met in the sacristy. Unlike the other rectory where we walked around freely, this rectory seemed to have different rules. And I quickly realized why.

Before our first visit, Marcus explained that the Bishop did not like people in the rectory. A priest's family members were ok and even that was to be in the rectory living room or common area. It was a huge "no no" to have someone in the private quarters. Now this was Marcus we are talking about. Rules and decorum did not translate well for him. The thrill of the chase was still alive and well, and to be honest, I was completely on board. It was one thing to get over on Mom and Dad or a Monsignor, but to get over on the Bishop...well that was exciting! I was all in. The plan was simple and clear and consistent. Meet in the sacristy before each visit. Enter the rectory through a long hallway connected to the Church. Stop. Look left and right several times, and when the high sign was given, scamper up the stairs and down the hall to Marcus' private quarters. I remember times when he would even point at the Bishop's door and laugh and quietly sneer. I did too because we were getting over. He was thoroughly enjoying himself. It was all one big colossal joke; too bad I was the punchline. Each visit began in his private sitting room, exchanging light banter sipping straight bourbon (don't forget, it was usually three in the afternoon). He would always sit close to me on the sofa, then take my hand and lead me into his bedroom. Standing next to the bed, he would hold me tight, and then pull me down to the floor. I would lie on my stomach (strangely enough, we never used the bed); he would unzip the zipper of my uniform skirt and pull it down below my hips, underwear too. Sometimes he would push up against me, sometimes not. I remember him putting his hand in between my legs and pushing my legs apart. As I laid face down bare butt, I remember him massaging my buttocks and outer thigh; sometimes to the point of physical pain. He added inner thigh rubbing to his repertoire along with gliding his hand across my clitoris. My body responded to this new behavior and I was frequently aroused. He never directly stimulated me; kind of like a passive-aggressive way of having sex. Looking back, I wonder if he justified my arousal as my own doing and not something he was directly responsible for. After all, it wasn't hardcore clit-rubbing or substantial penetration. Writing this now, I believe he took no ownership. I was at fault for being turned on, not him. As with most, if not all abuse survivors, I repeated this modeled behavior and did the same things to him that he did to me. When he would lie down on his stomach, he would unzip his own trousers and pull down his own underwear. I just realized now in writing this that he never allowed me to do that. He would spread his legs apart and I would rub his inner and outer thighs. He especially liked the inner thighs and the progression to his scrotum. He was not shy with his moans and grunts. He would gyrate his hips and at times lift his body off the floor so I could reach underneath him. And of course, the "you are such a good friend, you are such a good girl" patter. Most times, he would quickly and unexpectedly stand up and after reassembling his clothing, would usher me to the door. He would crack open the door and peer out down the hallway. I knew to stand perfectly still until I got the "hi" sign. When it was given, we would hurriedly walk past the Bishop's door and sneak downstairs through the church back to the sacristy. Done. There were times I got a quick goodbye hug and times when he would simply turn around and walk away. I never knew.

Several things were happening at this time of my life. Mom was becoming suspicious of my afternoon absences from home. I was not on a high school sports team, I wasn't always working at the rectory as much and when I would come home, I would usually go right upstairs. Can't blame her for being concerned. Anyway, one day I remember coming home from a Marcus visit to Mom sitting in the living room. That particular day, there was a funeral at Marcus' church and the sacristy

was full of incense. So I walk in the house drunk from bourbon and Mom demands that I come over to her. I was a little nervous, but mostly buzzed, so her stern tone didn't really concern me. She told me to lean over so she could smell me. "You've been smoking haven't you!!?" she said. I remember giving her this dipshit look and simply said, "No!" Now keep in mind I was hammered on bourbon, so if she could smell incense (or smoke as she thought it was) she could sure as hell smell bourbon. Nope. I was sent to my room without another word. I remember walking up the stairs to my bedroom gleefully thinking, "You dummy, I so got over on you!" I think I was grounded for smoking, but I didn't care. I was screwing with Mom and Dad left and right; something I knew Marcus was proud of. He directly told me how important it was to keep our secret; how no one would understand. And that all our special time would be taken away if someone found out. He was proud of me for not telling. One other time, I again came home loaded and Mom again asked me to come close. I was angry that day for some reason, and I refused. My behavior must have been pretty erratic, because half way up the stairs, I remember her following me and said, "Is anyone doing anything to you?" Well, I let out the most disrespectful nasty rant. "WHY WOULD YOU SAY THAT?" I remember saying. "NO, NOTHING IS HAPPENING!" That was the one and only time she asked me. Years later, she admitted guilt in not asking me over and over until I confessed. The truth is she could have asked me a thousand times, and I still would have said no.

Around this time I was also trying to do new things. The rectory wasn't the same since Marcus left, so I cut down my hours there. The CYO had a new coordinator, so that wasn't as big of a priority. What I really wanted were friends. My friend Tommy and I went to the same High School, but our best friend status was wavering. We didn't see each other as much and when we did it was mostly cordial. Weird. I remember noticing a distinct difference in him; how he walked, talked, dressed...practically everything. He wasn't the same person I buddied up with in grade school. Anyway, I didn't want rectory friends or CYO friends, just regular friends. I tried getting involved with school activities like softball and the school newspaper. I tried talking to kids outside of the tiny Honors classes I was in (which by the way were becoming more and more

> I REMEMBER THINKING THAT IF MY OWN GUIDANCE COUNSELOR DID NOT HAVE A SHRED OF FAITH IN ME..... THEN WHAT?

difficult). I really really tried. Looking back, it was probably like speaking Spanish in an English speaking world. I didn't know how to accumulate friends. Maybe my expectations were too high, or I wasn't interested in what they liked. I was also one step behind everyone else when it came to music and concerts and what was hip and happening. I was teased at times and called stupid and weird. I spent most of my high school years attached to a minute number of people and did anything and everything for them to like me.

Another new thing was girls. I began to realize I was attracted to females and wanted to pursue this further. Sure, no problem! This was the early 1980's...everyone was out doing it (sarcasm, of course). I remember looking at certain girls and female teachers and experiencing some of the same bodily reactions I had with Marcus; but without the touching. I was getting freaked out with the possibility (or probability) that I was gay. How could I know for sure? As fate would have it, it was around this time that Marcus took some of the old rectory rats "out." I remember that night very well. Marcus brought three or four of us out to a gay bar (my friend Tommy was with us). I remember walking in; it was dark, smoky and loud. The music was pounding. He walked us up to the bar and told us to sit. He ordered a variety of cocktails from scotch to bourbon to vodka and told us to see what we liked best (none of us knew what the hell we were doing) Sure, give a bunch of teenagers a plethora of alcohol! No sooner did the drinks arrive when Marcus mysteriously disappeared. Us kids made small talk and waited, and waited. I remember Tommy looking around nervously. He did not seem comfortable at all. I remember watching the "show." Young men, middle-aged men, older men; all holding hands and kissing in public. It was a sight I had never seen. Even though there were no women there that night, I felt comfortable with what I was seeing. I felt normal if that makes sense.

Along with the hundreds of men, there were dozens of posters and flyers on the walls about AIDS. Like most people at the time, I had heard of it, but didn't understand or really care about it. At that time, it was still thought to be transmitted on toilet seats, or kissing or even touching. I started getting freaked out. How on earth can I be here? On top of everything else in my life, I was now going to contract this deadly disease associated with the gay community. Shoot me now! I remember drinking my cocktail super-fast in an attempt to calm down. No one else seemed to care, so I decided to go back to having fun. I started to feel nauseous. The mixing of scotch and vodka and bourbon was turning into

a bad decision. I needed to use the bathroom. Marcus was still nowhere to be found, so I got up and wandered around looking for a place to throw up. I must have looked like a lost puppy because some very kind man asked, "Honey, are you ok?" "I need the bathroom," I said desperately trying not to vomit on this kind man's shoes. He maneuvered me through the crowded dance floor and put me outside the restroom door. Then he disappeared. I walked into this incredibly small bathroom and was overcome with more AIDS flyers on the walls. At this point, nausea and diarrhea were working hand in hand. I was paralyzed with fear. I did NOT want to sit down on THAT toilet or touch ANYTHING. My bodily functions took over and I gave in to excessive vomiting. I stood up, flushed the toilet and washed my hands with scorching hot water for several minutes. I even took a paper towel and opened the bathroom door so as not to touch the knob with my bare hand! Somehow I made it back to the bar and sat back with the other guys. Marcus finally reappeared to "retrieve" us (as I remember him calling it), and we left the bar and stumbled to the car. He was obviously drunk and we were obviously under age. We were far from licensed drivers. By the grace of God, he delivered us all home that night. Looking back, there were many times Marcus drove us while drunk. Whether it was a late night bar excursion, or an afternoon boat ride (Marcus owned a small boat on the Jersey Shore) liquor was always involved and always consumed to the max. One night while driving home from the shore, my friend Tommy noticed Marcus driving erratically. Just as the car nearly plowed into the cement toll booth on the Parkway, Tommy grabbed the steering wheel and readjusted the car's path. Marcus laughed. We laughed too, but later admitted we were scared to death. Anytime things seemed to be getting out of hand, Marcus would tell us to "Stop whining. Shut up and just have fun." And we did.

Dad's health continued to decline. Several ICU and CCU stays for days and weeks on end. As we never had "family meetings," my brother, sister and I were in the dark about the severity of Dad's condition. Looking back, I really believe Dad wanted to protect us. And I also believe Mom wanted to protect herself. She loved my father very much and other than typical marital squabbles, this was the guy she wanted to be with for life. To see him steadily deteriorate must have been shattering. She began spending more time out of the house with friends and coworkers. I guess we all needed to be out of the house more. Mom would go out "fraternizing" as Dad would call it, sometimes until the wee morning hours. Back then I was enraged with her behavior. "How could she leave

us?" I thought. Now I have a different take on it which I will expand on later. Frantic nights at the hospital became our way of life. Not that they happened every day or week, just often enough that when I began to feel secure and hopeful...really hopeful he would be ok, BAM...here we go again! Sometimes Dad was given a 50/50 chance of living or dying. Sometimes he was hooked up to every machine known to man and sometimes none. Sometimes I would leave his hospital room for a quick soda or snack and return to a deluge of nurses and doctors swarming over Dad. You just never knew. I told Marcus every chance I could about Dad, but he seemed to be less and less interested. At this point, Dad was dying... Mom was hardly ever home and my brother and sister were surviving as best they could. As much as I wanted and needed new things, I wanted Marcus to be that one constant.

Marcus was suddenly transferred again. Who knows the real reason why? The Church was notorious for reassigning priests to other parishes like it was a shuffleboard game. I knew of many priests who were pretty much uprooted and sent away. This time, Marcus's transfer was farther than ever, but by then I was driving, so the distance was not a huge problem. Visits continued. Visits intensified. I remember a party we were at one night at Patty's house (remember, the Adult Advisor we called about John). Patty had a small apartment with tiny rooms. Marcus showed up tipsy and the drinking continued through the night. I drank too. The liquor must have really lowered any inhibitions he had because in the middle of the hoopla, Marcus took my hand and led me into the bathroom. He closed the door behind us and practically fell into me. I was scared. He kissed my neck and began touching my back and buttocks. Then he turned around and stood with his hands clenching the sink, legs spread apart. I knew what he wanted. I began massaging his back and moved my hands downward to his buttocks. I remember hearing his belt buckle clanging in the darkness, which meant he had unzipped his pants. Then I heard a light thud. The pants hit the floor. This was, yet again, something new. I remember rubbing his buttocks over his underwear, then underneath. He was moaning the whole time, rhythmically moving his hips. He kept saying, "So relaxing." For the first time I slipped my hand through his underwear and began touching his penis and scrotum. I had only felt his hard penis through his clothing. Now it was the real deal. And it was the first male penis I had felt; the very first. His moans got louder and I remember laughing and telling him to quiet down. I don't think he climaxed, but he did enjoy the hand job.

After a few minutes, he pulled his pants back up, fastened his belt buckle, gave me a quick hug and opened the door. Did anyone know we were in the bathroom? Maybe not. Did anyone hear? Maybe. Considering how small that apartment was, and how long we were gone, it's really hard to believe no one knew.

Between Dad and Marcus, my grades were plummeting and warning notes from school became common. Remember those notes the school would send if you were in danger of failing? Yep, those were the ones. I think Mom was so overwhelmed with Dad's health (or lack thereof) that she had to prioritize. Getting through the day and keeping us safe, fed and clothed seemed more important than fighting with me over my grades. Besides, she probably thought my grades reflected my feelings about Dad. She was right; to an extent. I even failed health class my junior year...health class! I remember the teacher nonchalantly saying, "Sue, you failed my class, but I gave you a 'D'." Really nice of him. As I write this now, that was the year of a lot more graphic sex talk. Makes sense that I failed the class. I could give a shit about health class, or any class at that point. I was a mess. I dropped out of the Honors program and entered the "regular" classes. I think it was my guidance counselor's attempt to save my ass. I remember crying to her one day saying I did not understand ANY of this stuff. She told me to talk with my teachers. When I did, most were encouraging and supportive. One, however, was not. When I told her I wanted to drop her class for "regular" math, she was not happy. Her face turned to stone, and her words were cutting. "Do you REALLY think, Susan, you can just walk away from things when they get hard?" WOW! Uh...no I did not think that. I had a ton of hard things in my life. I WAS NOT walking away from THEM. She proceeded to lecture me on responsibility and commitment, and when she saw I was not looking to continue her class, she angrily dismissed me and said, "Fine, go tell Guidance." I most certainly did, and from that day, I was out of Honors. Regular classes were triple the size of my old ones, with kids I had only seen in the hallways. I was a lost guppy in an ocean of fish. I just wanted it to be over.

My one and only motivation to finish high school was a desire to be a teacher. I had wanted it since first grade. Mrs. Nash, my first grade teacher, was my idol and my assurance that teaching was it for me. In order to do that, I had to get into college, and in order to get into college I had to apply. One of the local colleges known for its teaching programs seemed like the perfect fit. It was very early senior year. I walked into the Guidance Office and asked my guidance counselor to send out the application which I proudly held in my hand. She was the same guidance counselor that signed me out of Honors classes, so you know this was not going to go well. She seemed preoccupied at first, looking down at papers. When she did focus on my request, she quickly looked up my current transcript. Purely based on that and with a look of "get away you're wasting my time" she said, and I quote, "Why are you bothering with this? You will never get in." I stood there as if in a dream, like I would wake up and poof...be living in my dorm room curling my roommate's hair like in the commercials. I guess I didn't leave the office promptly enough because she seemed annoyed I was still standing there. I said I wanted to be a teacher. Again, she gave me a look. I begged her to mail the application. As God is my witness, I remember her snatching the application out of my hand saying, "Fine!" I stood there shaking. The way she took that application from me with such disregard. The building could have been on fire at that point and I would not have noticed. I remember thinking that if my own guidance counselor did not have a shred of faith in me... then what? That one experience, that one encounter could have broken me beyond repair. Going home and telling Mom and Dad much of anything with school was very different than it is now. And even if I told my parents, what could they have done? I do remember praying harder than ever in my life, asking God to please, please make this happen. I knew in my core I would be a good teacher, I just needed the degree to prove it. It was months before I got a response.

When the envelope finally came, it was big and bulky; a good sign, I was told, because the acceptances had all the information about books, housing, etc. Mine was big and bulky! Hallelujah! I got in! Can't remember if I went back to tell her, but she must have known. After all, her job was to "counsel" all of us youngsters, right! I was on cloud nine! This was the biggest accomplishment of my life. Considering all my struggles with reading and keeping up (and everything ELSE happening) this was my time to show that I was no dummy. For high school graduation, Mom and Dad gave me a beautiful gold crucifix ring. I had my eye on it for some time and somehow they came up with the money to buy it. Thanks Mom and Dad...I don't know how you did it. Anyway, I remember being out with Marcus one night, somehow ending with him driving me home. I showed him the ring and asked if he would bless it. As he was driving, he lifted his right hand and placed it over the ring and began to pray, "Heavenly father, please bless this ring and please bless

Susan." He then emphatically motioned the sign of the cross over the ring saying, "In the name of the Father, the Son and the Holy Spirit...Amen." No sooner did he bless my ring than he slid that same hand between my legs. I guess that hand had done worse.

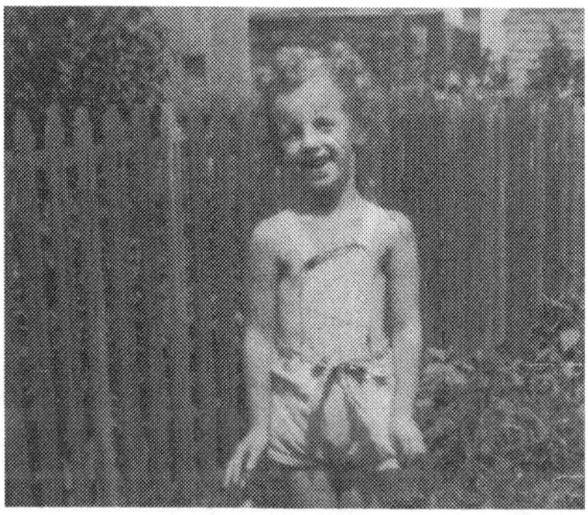

Mom age 4

Dad age 7

Mom and Aunt Reggie

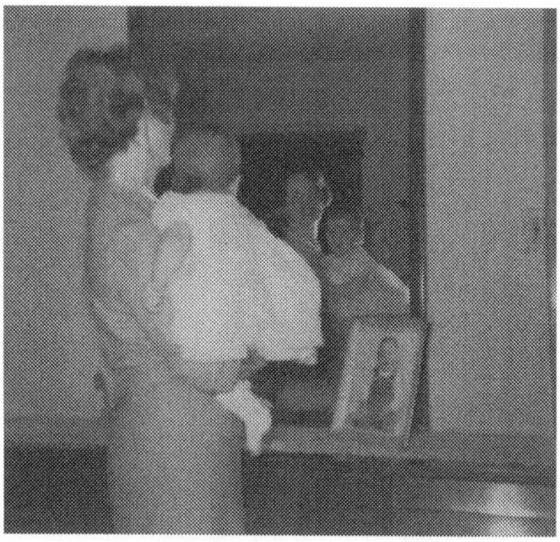

Mom and I

My sister's christening

The early days

8th Grade graduation

Dad, Grandmom and Mom

Lots of drinking to get by...

Me being the "good teacher"

Me and Mom...after she knew

Me and Mom...after she knew

CHAPTER SIX
BLESSED ARE THOSE WHO MOURN...

The summer after high school graduation was one big blur. I went out a lot and drank a lot. I was working at a local jewelry shop on the weekends to make extra money. Marcus was transferred yet again, and this time was made a pastor of a church even farther than the one before. I remember visiting for the first time; his residence was twice the size as ones in the past and was decorated to the hilt. Being a pastor I'm sure had its advantages; one of which was having more control of parish monies. Now, I am not accusing, or even surmising (well, maybe I am surmising). All I can say is there was a lot more "stuff," with a lot more booze and a lot more people. New car, new clothes (I had become good at noticing what he wore). He was going places. I only saw him a couple of times that summer, and when I did, I was introduced to lots of different people. Our intimate group of misfits was now a massive group of "it" people. I remember feeling kind of cast away; once this "special girl" now just a number that you hold at the bakery. I was not happy. Marcus, on the other hand, was king. He made grand entrances into his sitting quarters wearing flamboyant wraps and shoes. He sat in this Queen Anne style chair (or as we dubbed it King Anne) and demanded guests sit at his feet (no, really). He had certain people mix drinks and others answer the door. He was completely in charge.

College was a perfect fit. I remember buying school supplies little by little that summer. I bought whatever new wardrobe I could. Man, was I excited! I was put on a wait list for housing, so I began college life as a commuter. My first day of school was actually the second day because, as with high school, I was absent my first day with a hangover. The alcohol was now my closest friend. I left the house that morning with a knapsack and homemade lunch and twenty-five cents. Since I only had twenty-five cents, I had the need to 'bring my own'. I'm sure Mom and Dad would have given me more, but I wanted to do it all myself. I arrived at school early, and found parking difficult; impossible really. I remember driving around getting more and more nervous that I would be late to my first class. In the corner of my eye was a sliver

of a parking space, and I jumped at it. I parked my car and ran across campus frantically. Made it to class just in time. That day was so exhilarating! This was unlike anything I had imagined! Thousands of students of every ethnicity and culture. Classes at all times of the day. No class bells or late warnings. You were in charge of you. Grown up stuff. I must have had a full day of classes because it was late afternoon when I left. I looked out at the once packed parking lot seeing fewer cars than that morning. Problem was my car was one of the fewer! My car was gone! I distinctly remember thinking "holy fuck" but then collecting myself and coming up with a logical conclusion; I was in the wrong lot. So I wandered around for at least an hour from parking lot to parking lot, praying I would spot that light blue Dodge Duster. No Duster. When I returned to the first lot, I accepted the inevitable. Now the question was, "What the heck to I do now?" Somehow I found campus police, and they told me the process of how and where to pick up my car. They even let me use their phone to call my father; didn't have to use my twenty-five cents! Dad was super ill and super angry. Who could blame him? He had to drive forty minutes to pick me up, another ten to the impound lot, and produce close to one hundred dollars! Looking back, his anger dissipated quickly and there was no wrath or judgment. I owed him a lot that day. This was not the start I had hoped for.

MY BROTHER CAME IN FIRST FOLLOWED BY MOM AND MY SISTER. HE TOSSED THE KEYS ON THE TABLE, CAME OVER TO ME, WRAPPED HIS ARMS AROUND ME AND SAID "IT WAS QUICK AND IT WAS PAINLESS". DAD WAS GONE

That first week of college, I realized I needed to work harder than I ever did before in my school life. Whether it was my reading/ comprehension disability or the mounting pressures of Dad's illness or all the shit with Marcus, I could not remember much of anything. I figured out that I had to read things three times to really retain the information. First time was straight reading, second was highlighting and third was note-taking. And that was for every single thing I read in my undergrad studies. What took most people an hour to complete took me several hours. At first I was inconsolable, feeling more stupid than ever, and certain I would never become a teacher. It was hard studying at home because Dad was usually coughing or sleeping; either one of those could warrant an emergency trip to the hospital. I kept my eye on the prize if you will, and trudged ahead. A few weeks into school I was accepted for student housing. That was a good day. I remember getting the letter in the morning with a move-in date for the following week. I started packing...well...piling clothes and stuff. I wanted out in the worst way, and the Universe granted my wish. The day came for me to move in. And I was all alone. No family or friends offered, or were available to help me. I carried box after box after box after box through the campus parking lot, up three flights of stairs (the freshman dorm at the time had no elevator). It was late afternoon into the evening. It's funny how nowadays students have an entourage of folks helping them move into school...buying them dorm stuff from their registry; not me. My parents did not understand my need to live at school (aka, a waste of money) so they did not buy me much. Kind of sad now that I reflect back. Very sad, actually. I was always there for other people giving my guts away. Why weren't they there for me? After hours and countless treks to my car, I was in my new home. With my unicorn pictures on my wall, and my cheesy bedspread neatly in place, I was home. My roommate came in later that night and we briefly chatted. We were cordial, but that was it. She was intelligent and well off. I was not. She must have spoken to the RA because within that first week, she moved out. I went through several roommates looking back. I guess I really was that slow geeky kid. I only came home on weekends to work at the jewelry store. That was my spare money for food, phone bill, etc. I distinctly remember when I first told Mom about moving on campus. The only thing she said was, "Don't think I will ever pay for your phone bill. That's all on you!" Years later she apologized profusely for her crappy comment and explained she was scared her children were beginning to leave. I understood later, but at the time it really was crappy. And I never missed paying a phone bill!

Freshman and sophomore years came and went. I was away from home and away from Dad's continuing demise. He was visibly getting worse and I wanted nothing to do with it. I was free at school to do everything I wanted. I dated lots and LOTS of guys and had lots of "experiences." As I often refer to it, "I had many satisfied customers." Even though I felt so comfortable in the gay bars with my friends and Marcus, I still wasn't completely sure I was gay or wanted to be gay for that matter. I was trying so hard to be normal; in other words, trying to be straight. Although attracted to females for years now, I did not have my first lesbian encounter until a couple of years later.

When I would go home on the weekends and see Marcus, yet another

new dynamic ensued. I remember being at a party with Marcus. He greeted me a bit coldly, and then whisked me outside. Tending bar was a handsome well-built man. He had dark brown hair and a gorgeous smile. I remember Marcus asking him to make me a drink and then whispering something into his ear. The guy smiled and looked at me. A second later, Marcus whispered to me that I should go with this guy. Marcus said he liked me and wanted to get to know me."Wait, what?" I remember thinking. I had just gotten to the party and wanted to mingle and chill. I remember being confused, but then as if on autopilot, I agreed. Marcus walked away and began talking with some younger male guests (I was now part of the older crowd). The bartender asked if I wanted to go talk. Somehow we found our way to his car and he went straight for it. He started kissing me and sticking his tongue down my throat. His hands were up my shirt as he guided my hand to his erect penis. He was moaning. I was trained well, so I proceeded to unzip his pants and expose him. I went down on him like a champ. He was groaning and gyrating his hips...sound familiar? He was also rubbing my back and reaching around to rub my front. After a brief time, he came. I pretended to finish the deed, but cleverly spit out his semen on his car floor. No holding, no kiss, no nothing; just a smile and a re-zipping of his pants and it was back to the party. He didn't even say "thank you." I remember seeing Marcus again and he gave me this eerie wink; kind of like, "Hey, way to go!!" That was the first of several of Marcus' orchestrated liaisons at several parties. Each time, he would tell me to go with some random guy, and each time I dutifully agreed. Years later, one of my therapists said he was prostituting me out. "He was your pimp," I remember her saying. I was infuriated she spoke so poorly of him and even more upset that she viewed me as a prostitute. I rejected her theory completely. Marcus loved ME. I was HIS special girl. Now I believe she was spot on. She explained her theory this way: Marcus was becoming "interested" in others; therefore, he maintained his hold over me by loaning me out. All the while knowing I was still his, when HE decided. Marcus was a master manipulator; of people, and of circumstances. He even used his own family for self-gain. There was another party hosted by his older eccentric uncle. His home was a big beautiful turn-of-the-century mansion. The man had money. We were outside in the courtyard drinking and dancing. I watched Marcus make his uncle have drink after drink (as he did with Monsignor's special coffee), and once his uncle began to stumble, Marcus and another guy walked him into the house upstairs to his bedroom. A few minutes later,

Marcus reappeared outside laughing and smiling. When I approached him, he said, "SHHH...we just took money from my uncle!" A friend later confirmed that Marcus took his uncle's wallet out of his back pocket before resting him on the bed and emptied most of it before returning outside. That was a poignant moment for me. If someone could take such pleasure in stealing from his own flesh and blood, stealing and raping and abusing other people was nothing. As buzzed as I was that night, I remember looking at him with a different lens. I am forever grateful that these random encounters I had with men did not lead to pregnancy or AIDS. I hooked up with many men in many places; all arranged by Marcus.

Junior and senior year, I decided to move back home and commute. I wasn't gelling with any of my roommates and always felt like the round peg in the square hole. And some let me know it. Money was an issue, I admit, but by then my fear of being around Dad was shifting to a need to be close to him. I can't explain exactly what happened, I just knew time was short. When I told him I was moving home to be closer to him he laughed at me and said, "Come on....really?" I was crushed. I was sacrificing my freedom to be with him if he needed me and this is what he chose to say? Dad wasn't exactly the best communicator and did not show clear raw emotions until the end. Maybe he knew my moving back was a solidifier of his inevitable end. Whatever the reason, it hurt. It would have been nice to hear, "Thank you for being here" or "I love you." Mom and Dad didn't interact much at all; Mom did her thing, Dad his. So I kept the pattern going and hunkered down with school work and a part-time social life. School, work, student teaching and working part time all made for a very busy life, but still, when Marcus called, I would go. I know this makes no rational sense, but by this time I was fully groomed and programmed. Will get into more of that later. One of the last physical encounters I had with Marcus came when he was in his last parish as the pastor. He had again been transferred. He had a beautiful suite; living room, bedroom and bar (of course). It was here one day that the usual laying down on the floor happened, but with a twist. We had our pattern; friendly cocktails and make our way to his bedroom. It was dark. As always, he motioned me to lie on the floor. This time he lay on top of me. All two hundred fifty pounds or so of him was on top of me. I remember him shifting his weight and hearing the clang of his belt buckle. I heard his zipper unzip. I heard the belt buckle and the pants unzip. He then stretched his arms over his head in front of me (like a Superman pose). He began pressing his weight into me more and more. He was moaning. I remember wincing in pain and praying to God my ribs would not shatter. I was certain my ribs would shatter. At some point he braced his arms and began gyrating. I felt an unusual twitching of his body. He let out a loud groan, and his arms gave way. He had cum. I knew because I felt wetness on the back of my pants I had never felt before. He then stood up, refastened his clothes and walked away. He did not help me up this time or give me a celebratory hug. He got what he wanted. Dad and I were spending more time together and in my greatest hopes and delusions I thought he was getting better. He told me stories about growing up and about his parents and things like being in the Air Force in Korea. He talked about courting and marrying Mom. All this from a guy who I barely knew up until that time! But I didn't care; I was actually enjoying the time. He became fun to be around and I loved getting to know my Dad. I felt connected with him, and I think he felt the same. Then one day he came home from a doctor's appointment. He looked scared. "Come on, the doctor said I have to go to the hospital now." He hurried into his bedroom and collected some underwear and other clothes. I was in a daze at first, since he had had a pretty good run health-wise. I sprang up from the couch and began helping him. He asked me to call Mom at work. We got to the emergency room where Dad "checked in." I knew that emergency room far too well. I remember him sitting in the intake chair looking thin and pale. He was signing some papers, hands trembling. You would think after eight years of this I would be desensitized to it all. Piece of cake, right? Trust me... never the case. I did everything I could not to hyperventilate and pass out. I was terrified, and I was alone. The nurse quickly took Dad away and I was instructed to stay in the ER and wait to hear where exactly Dad was. So I waited, and waited and waited. Mom arrived, and we sat together making small talk. She had been through so much. I remember getting out of my chair a hundred times with nervousness. Mom was growing agitated with my behavior. "Susan, why don't you just go?" Didn't have to ask me twice. I was gone. When I got home I was there alone. I sat in Dad's recliner and cried. I started regretting my decision to move back. I DID NOT want to go through this. Mom arrived home late that night and told me Dad was in CCU. We sat together in the TV room.

I visited Dad several times that week. He looked "good" and was laughing and talking. They moved him to the CCU "step-down" unit (always a good sign). Each day, they took him off more and more

machines. More good. I remember seeing him one day sharing sour balls and discussing his plans for coming home. It was just he and I in the quiet room; no machines buzzing or beeping. He hugged me goodnight and I told him I would see him the next morning. When the next morning came, I woke up happy and full of hope. Dad was off all machines and was coming home soon. When I got to his room, he was again hooked up to machines, nurses and a doctor surrounding him. He had a "bad night." I remember looking at him in disbelief; and he looking at me the same way. He smiled and said, "Honey, it's okay." I bolted. I could not see him one more day, one more minute hooked up to every machine known to man. If you have not gone through this, it is utterly terrifying. "How is this happening," I remember thinking. He was "fine" the night before. Of course, he was never really fine, but that's what I had convinced myself. I somehow made it home that day and kept busy.

The next day was a Sunday. Mom must have called my brother because he was home that morning. We decided to visit Dad in shifts, so Mom and my brother and sister went that morning and afternoon and I was supposed to go later. Looking back, I tried to convince myself I was going back; the truth was I knew I could not see Dad one more time with all those machines. I went shopping with my friend Jeannie. We had a great afternoon and she dropped me off to an empty house and went home. Weird part was, about ten minutes later, she called and said she wanted to come over. "But we just hung out," I said. "Yeah, I know," she said, "But it's still early." Oh well, I thought, I liked her, so why not. When she arrived, she sat down next to me and told me the real reason for her return. Mom had left a message on her home message machine asking her to stay with me. Dad was in critical condition, and Mom did not want me to be alone. She also did not want me to drive, so if I wanted to come to the hospital, she asked Jeannie to bring me. "Do you want to go," I remember her asking. That was THE toughest question I was ever presented with. Did I want to see my father? Of course I did! Did I want to see my father hooked up to bell and whistle machines watching him breathe (or not breathe)? "No," I replied. "Unless he asks for me, if not, then no." She tried to prepare me for future guilt and regret if I didn't see him, but none of that mattered. I could not handle it anymore. The years of such living were traumatic and beyond repair. Jeannie accepted my decision and we stayed at my house, drinking some disgusting super sweet liquor. To this day, I cannot stand the smell of fruity liquor! My family came home later that night and said it was in God's hands,

plain and simple. Mom thanked Jeannie for staying with me. Jeannie hugged me and left. There was total silence. My mother, brother, sister and I just stared into space. None of us wanted or needed to talk. Everyone was exhausted. I remember praying the phone would not ring, especially in the middle of the night. Those phone calls had happened before, and they were never good. It did not ring.

The next day my family chose to go back to the hospital, I again chose not to. They seemed to understand. Instead, I went to the church where I first met Marcus, the church where I worked as a "rectory rat." I walked in and knelt before the Blessed Mother statue. I sobbed, talked, and pleaded, prayed, sobbed some more. I lit so many candles, thinking the volume of candles lit would help the situation. I will never forget looking up at the statue and saying out loud, "Either make him better or take him...I can't handle this anymore." I returned home to an empty house. It was early evening. Good news I thought. Around eight o'clock pm, I heard the back door open. My brother came in first followed by Mom and my sister. He tossed the keys on the table, came over to me, wrapped his arms around me and said , "It was quick and it was painless." Dad was gone. We all just sat there at first, staring off into space. And then the tears came. Mom was catatonic, but suddenly asked me to get her little phone book. The gut wrenching phone calls began. The first person she called was her sister, my Aunt Reggie (remember the one who wanted to beat up the girls for calling them crazy?) One after one, she called aunts and uncles and friends, each call harder to hear than the one before. My brother was sitting in Dad's recliner, and at one point said, "It's like I'm living in a house without a roof." What a profound way to express his vulnerability around losing his father. Aunt Reggie was the only one allowed to come to the house that night. She was there for Mom and we were there for ourselves.

In planning the funeral, we discussed the wake and the mass. I asked my family if Marcus should preside. "Oh, sure," Mom said. "He is such a good man." Keep in mind; not one person knew the truth about Marcus and I intended to keep it that way. The wakes were held at a funeral home right next to the church and school where I first met Marcus. And the priests' residences were the building next to that. Those same rooms where a whole lot happened. The wakes were well-attended and were as lovely as wakes could be. Many people spoke highly of Dad and I got to hear stories about him I never knew. There was laughter and fond memories. I needed that. The number of people who came in and out still floors me to this day. A lot of love there. The morning of Dad's funeral, we went into see him one last time. Mom stood over Dad for quite a while, reluctant to sit down when I guided her to her chair. My brother, sister and I going through the motions. People started to arrive and the greetings and "thank you for coming" began again. After a brief prayer by the priest (Marcus) we were asked to file by the casket. First, friends and neighbors, then aunts, uncles and cousins, then immediate family. I remember standing next to Mom holding her up. She didn't want to leave Dad. My brother, sister, mother and I all sobbed and walked into the adjoining room to wait to proceed to the church. Mom was a wreck and I did everything I could to take care of her. As we waited, I saw Jeannie standing in the hallway in front of me (the friend who was with me that Sunday). She smiled and put her head down. I was glad she was there. Then we were told to stand and follow the casket as we proceeded to the church. We walked outside the funeral home and through the parking lot. We walked right past the priests' residences. Even though Marcus had not been there for several years, a flood of memories overwhelmed me. I remember walking behind my father's casket looking up at the window of the room I was in many times; never for a holy reason. I shook my head and blinked my eyes. I had to focus on what was in front of me...literally. We entered church to the song, "On Eagle's Wings." There was Marcus midway down the aisle waiting for Dad's casket. He began a prayer and blessed the casket with incense. He was a freak for incense, overusing it whenever possible. Remember when I came home and Mom thought I was smoking? Incense! We then took our seats and proceeded through the mass. Marcus gave a crappy homily spewing about good times and fond memories of "Moe" (Dad's nickname). All crap! As I sat there, I remembered a time Marcus promised to visit Dad during one of his hospital stays. Dad had the nurses bathe him early that morning and then he waited. And waited. Marcus never came. When I got there late that afternoon, Dad was disappointed and sad. He was so looking forward to his company. I was livid. How could he leave my father waiting there? It took me years to get over the anger of that broken promise. When I finally told my family about Marcus and the abuse, my sister expressed anger over him presiding at Dad's funeral service. "How could you let him preach at my father's funeral when all that was going on?!" she said. In other words, "Susan, you stupid pathetic moron, how could you let that happen?" On some level, she was justified in feeling that way; but grooming and programming do not compete with clear rational thinking.

It is not that simple.

After the funeral at the repass there was lots of drinking and eating, but mostly drinking. The VFW guys were there playing bartender. The Polish food warmed the room. Mom did an amazing job not only with the planning of the repast, but also allowing us to grieve in our own way. My brother and sister and I went into the back room and played pool like we did when we visited Dad as Commander of the VFW. It was our way of celebrating him and she knew that. When a family member questioned the appropriateness of us doing such things on this somber day, Mom came right to our defense. I remember her looking me in the eyes saying, "You kids do whatever you need to do." God, what a gift! So much stress and pent-up trauma allowed to be released by a pool game. When we got home that day, it was incredibly quiet. We knew there would be no more hospital phone calls and no more sprints to Dad's bedside. It was surreal. It was an atmosphere I had not had for the last eight years. Now what?

CHAPTER SEVEN
AND THEN THERE WAS LIGHT...

The year after Dad died, there was movement; lots of movement. I graduated from college and got my state teaching certificate. I was certified...in a good way! I started sending out resumes and showing up at administrators' doors with a smile and a promise I would make "an outstanding addition to their school district." I had that line down pat. Without my knowledge and much to my disdain, Mom called an old high school friend of hers who happened to be Superintendent of Schools in a local school district. Bing, bang, boom...my first teaching job, three months after graduation. Looking back I am forever grateful she made that phone call, but I gave her hell for it then! I remember my first day of my first real job. I was a full time Kindergarten teacher in a small urban school district. It was "Welcome Back Day" for staff with the students arriving the next day. A day of meet and greets, department meetings and putting the finishing touches on our classrooms. I looked great! I wore a royal blue skirt, a pink silk blouse and high heel blue shoes. Too bad the rest of the teachers were wearing shorts, jeans and flip flops! I had no way of knowing the "first day" was super casual. Yep, I was the newbie. We sat in the school library listening to the building principal discuss protocol and expectations. We went through main office procedures and lunch duties. This was my new life. At the end of the meetings, we were allowed to go to our classrooms for last touch-ups. I had been in there several times after first being hired; only this day was my last day as a novice. I remember smelling the new crayons and admiring my organizational skills. As I shut off the lights to go home, I said to myself, "Tomorrow is the best day of my life!"

The first day of school for the kids was nothing short of a shit show. Kids, parents and teachers everywhere! Kids screaming for their mothers, teachers annoyed with incomplete rosters. The principal scurrying from room to room. Poor guy probably lost five pounds in water weight that day! I had thirty kids on my roster. That's right...thirty. AND two sets of twins...AND one little girl who screamed so loud she chose to sit in the corner the whole day. Come to think of it, she sat in that corner all month!

The room was only big enough for about twenty kids, but I was told to make it work. I was fortunate to have a classroom assistant, so she helped me seat the children and acclimate them to their new surroundings. I remember announcing to the class who I was and how much fun we were going to have. I remember giving the children paper and new crayons and telling them to draw a special picture for their families. I remember bending down and making sure to compliment each child's artwork. And I distinctly remember seeing what appeared to be a bug fall out of one little girl's hair onto her drawing paper. Yep, she had lice. My assistant located the school nurse and when she came in to evaluate the situation, she concluded almost a dozen students had lice (an infestation she called it). ARE YOU KIDDING ME! The best day of my life, my ass! Now what? The nurse explained that every child with lice needed to go home immediately and needed to report back to her the next day and be checked for reentry into school. As the nurse was leaving, I followed her into the hall and asked her to check my hair just to be safe. You know where this is going. I had lice too. My warm compassionate hugs I gave to the crying children those first few minutes of school were coming back to haunt me. The nurse said under the current health guidelines, I had to leave the room immediately and go home (considering I missed my first days of high school and college, this seemed apropos, don't you think?). I stood in the hallway processing what had just happened. She started walking to the Main Office to inform the principal and I started walking back into my classroom to gather my things. "You can't go in there," she exclaimed. "What?" I said, "I need my stuff." "We will get it for you. Wait right there." I could not go into MY classroom to get MY stuff. My assistant heard the discussion and came out to investigate. She then went to my desk, got my coat and book bag, handed them to me and said, "See you tomorrow." I stopped at the drug store and bought some anti-lice crap. When Mom came home from work, she asked how my first day was. What could I do except laugh and tell her. I think we both drank scotch that night!

The next day after a complete lice treatment, I was back at school. Just like the kids, I had to report to the nurse before I could reenter my classroom. She was in the teachers' room eating a bagel. When I peeked in, asking if I could see her, she looked at the clock and said, "It's not my time to start yet. I'll see you in a few minutes." I paced the hallway waiting. When she finally emerged, we went down to her office for a check over. "Uh oh," I remember her saying. "You

have to go home again." This could not be happening. I told her I followed the lice crap directions to the letter. "Did you wash your clothes," she said. "No," I replied. She explained that lice jump and they probably got on my clothes and jumped wherever and found their way back to my hair. SO disgusting. And actually now funny as I remember all this. What a way to start my career! Mom could not believe I was home for day two. Neither could I. The good news is by day three, I was back at school because on day two every piece of clothing I owned and all my bedding was washed in hot water and vinegar. My colored clothes were a little dull, but damn it, they were lice free!

Things didn't get much better after that. I was edgy and defiant. I was not working well with my principal and administrators. Well, let me clarify. I was always to work on time (or early). I turned in my lesson plans and required paperwork on or before the deadlines. It wasn't any of bookkeeping stuff. I was resentful of any authority figure and resentful of being told what to do. I was "young and dumb" as I refer to it, but it was more than that. I REALLY despised being told how to run my classroom. And I let them know it. I had a couple administrators work with me with sample teaching lessons. My principal came in early one morning and sat me down to explain "the way things should be." He was a kind, fatherly guy. Looking back, he didn't have to do that. The truth was they were all trying a lot harder than I was. Mom tried to help me, too. She had worked in corporate America for years and tried to help me understand how to navigate the waters. I wasn't listening. Towards the end of that first year, one of the secretaries I was friendly with showed me a letter "in my file." It was from my supervisor to the superintendent. I remember the wording: "Please do not call Susan in right away as I will continue to work with her." Translation: Do not fire Susan after only one year until you hear back from me. You would think after seeing this, my attitude would have made a 360 degree turn. Nope.

WHEN SHE ASKED ME TO TELL HER ABOUT MYSELF, I REALLY DIDN'T KNOW WHERE TO START. I DIDN'T THINK I HAD A TRAUMATIC CHILDHOOD AND NOTHING REALLY BAD HAPPENED TO ME (OR SO I THOUGHT)

Year two started with no lice, but my same crappy attitude. I was being observed more and my supervisor had me to her office numerous times to "work with me." It wasn't until one of my fellow teachers spoke to me that I got the message loud and clear. It was an in-service training day for staff. I was in the hallway with Rose and was loudly proclaiming my disdain for one particular administrator. I was bitching and moaning about a litany of things that were wrong and stupid. I guess she had heard enough because I remember her gently taking my shoulders and putting me up against the wall. Seriously, putting up on the wall! She stared into my eyes and spoke softly yet sternly, "You will talk like them, you will walk like them, you will do EVERYTHING they say to do...and you will smile and thank them for their help." She continued, "You worked hard to get here, and you're throwing it all away. It's nobody's fault but your own." It clicked. I was not going to live my dream of being a teacher with my crappy attitude. She was right. From that day on, I talked and walked and did everything THEY told me. My contract was renewed and I eventually got tenure.

Now there's a contributing reason why that first year was so hard. Sometime that fall, I was at Marcus' for yet another drunken soirée. I remember walking into his private residence and being surprised to see more new faces, several young faces, including two young boys I had not met before. They were brothers, and sons of current parishioners. Nice boys; cute, respectful, and, just like me when I was younger, getting loaded. Boy, did this look familiar. I remember Marcus sitting in that King Anne chair wearing this huge bright blue ring on his left hand. He displayed it proudly to all of us, as if he were a king holding court. Mostly, I remember the boys sitting at Marcus' feet, one on his left, and one on his right. They were about thirteen and sixteen. I remember the younger boy looking up at Marcus as if he really was a king, eyes wide and in awe. Marcus was stroking the hair of the younger boy, staring down at him with that same smile, the same smirking glare he had given me. I could not stop staring. It was like I was watching my life movie, only this time they were the stars. The older brother got up at one point and was throwing up in the bathroom (too much alcohol). When Marcus was told of the boy's "illness" he looked annoyed, but got up to assist. I struck up a conversation with the younger one. He told me how his parents were out of town that weekend and how happy they were that Father was watching over them. With a huge smile he said, "We are staying here this weekend until my parents get home." "Here with relatives?" I asked. "No, here in the rectory with Father." A light bulb went off in my head. More like a neon sign saying, "Danger, danger." For the very first time, I started to question my life with Marcus. Marcus came back to the party and sat

back down on his throne. He continued stroking the boy's hair and smiling downward. When the boy asked about his older brother, Marcus made a joke (of course) and said he would be fine. He said he was resting on his bed. Then I got sick to my stomach. Marcus shot me a look and gave me one of his twisted smiles and winks. I was confused and angry. Ok, so he had these young friends. Ok, so he seemed to be quite friendly with these young brothers. How could I even THINK what was happening was wrong? Just like the going-to-confession discussion in the rectory years before, I felt guilty and ashamed for thinking so poorly about Marcus. I left the party that night looking back at the young brothers nearly passed out on the floor. It was the last party I attended.

Work was going better considering I was now a full team player. A co-worker told me about a Master's program she was thinking of enrolling in. I had absolutely NO plans to go back to school, and I initially paid her no mind. Then I started to question being a classroom teacher for the next thirty years. I loved teaching and loved the kids, but did not love the constraints and the judgment. Maybe there was something else I could do with children. When I asked to see her course catalog, the next chapter in my life was there in black and white: Graduate Degree in Counselor Education. I could stay in the public schools, but have more independence and flexibility. And I could REALLY help kids and feel special (sound familiar?). The need to feel special along with almost total reimbursement from my school district made my decision to enroll in Graduate School an easy one. I again became a full-time college student.

During one early class, our assignment was to attend private therapy. Three sessions. The rationale was simple: the best way to counsel others is to know what the therapy experience feels like and not project any of our own "stuff" on our clients. If I was going to be a counselor/therapist, I had to be present one hundred percent for other people. I called a local therapist and arranged a meeting. The therapist was kind and soft-spoken. When she asked me to tell her about myself, I really didn't know where to start. I didn't think I had a traumatic childhood and nothing really bad happened to me (or so I thought). She asked me to talk about past relationships and I proceeded to tell her about Marcus. I was matter-of-fact. I remember her listening intently and taking notes. When I paused, she looked at me and asked how I felt about being sexually abused. Wait... abused? I was not abused! This was NOT one of THOSE things you heard that happened to other people. She calmed me down and suggested we meet again later that week to keep the flow going. I was offended and thought she was way off the mark, but I agreed. The second session, she zeroed in on Marcus and asked several questions. What began as a classroom assignment was turning into an odyssey of self-discovery. She proceeded to explain the dynamics of sexual molestation and how perpetrators groom and program their victims. I wanted NOTHING to do with this conversation. She was a whack job, and did not know me at all. How dare she not only judge me, but judge Marcus! Fuck her! I left that day not booking a third session. When I got home, I tried to forget about things and focus on my graduate work. I came across the assignment sheet for the three counseling sessions. I needed the therapist's signature stating I attended. Crap! I really didn't want to find someone new. I had to go back. It was just one more time. My plan was to not take any of it seriously, get her to sign my assignment sheet and say goodbye. I called her and scheduled another appointment.

At our last session, the therapist asked me if I had been having anger/depression/anxiety in the last few years. Wait, how would she know that? When I said "yes" she again proceeded to explain the effects of sexual abuse. For some reason, my resentment and disdain for her softened and I allowed myself to hear her. I had been angry with Marcus after seeing him with the young boys, and I had been questioning our relationship prior to seeing this woman. She was not off the mark at all. And she was the one and only person who knew the truth about Marcus. Believe it or not, I asked if I could continue to see her and talk more about my "stuff." She graciously agreed. After about two months and a lot of tears and self-deprecating, she suggested I do three things: set up a meeting with the Diocesan Bishop, retain an attorney (she provided me a name), and tell my family. My meeting with the Bishop was to inform him of the abuse and protect myself if the church was, in her words, "less than helpful." She shared a couple of similar experiences she had had with other clients; and let's just say they did not go well. She explained that the Bishop was responsible for keeping his people safe (especially the children) and that Marcus could not be allowed to continue his ministry. Retaining an attorney was to protect myself. I admit I was offended with her suggestion that I needed to "protect myself" but she was on the money about other things; maybe she had insight there, too. Finally, tell my family. Wow. That was nowhere on my radar. Mom had been through enough losing Dad the year earlier, and I was not emotionally ready to provide her details of the abuse (I was finally calling it what it was). I remember feeling absolute panic and sickness. Looking back it was guilt, too.

I was ratting Marcus out. Can you imagine...I felt bad for telling about Marcus. Another classic programming move. The victim often covers up and lies when asked about abuse in order to protect the perpetrator (remember when Mom asked me if anyone hurt me and I denied it?) I was also afraid of unraveling more stuff. So much had happened with my therapist and me in that two months. Her time and role in my life were brief and poignant. She emphasized that I had been molested and that what happened was NOT okay and NOT dismissible. By not taking action with the Church I was in some way allowing it to continue. I left her office that day and cried and prayed and cried some more. I didn't tell a soul. The first thing I decided to do was tell the Bishop.

CHAPTER EIGHT
AND THE TRUTH SHALL SET YOU FREE...

Home alone and with my heart jumping out of my skin, I dialed the phone to the Bishop's Office. I decided before that call to hold off on calling an attorney, thinking and believing this could be settled "in house." Simple enough, right? I would tell them everything and they would help me. I was put on hold and transferred several times, each time producing more and more anxiety. Finally, I was connected to the Diocesan Director of Personnel, Father Brentley. He told me he was the Bishop's secretary; a liaison between the Bishop and the people. I nervously began the conversation with my request to meet with the Bishop. When he asked the nature of the meeting, I began to provide specifics. My emotions overwhelmed me and I was sobbing and stammering. He quickly interrupted and said, "I do not need to know intimate details." I remember those words. Well, didn't he want to know the nature of my meeting with the Bishop? In any case, he sounded empathetic and assured me the Church, and especially the Bishop, were extremely concerned. "We want to help you, "I remember him saying, and assured me a meeting would take place with the Bishop "very soon." He told me he would call back in a day or two with a meeting date. Since I had my own phone line and my own answering machine that sounded fine. I remember hanging up the phone feeling some relief, but greater fear of what might be ahead. Keep in mind, I was still living at home, and I hadn't told my mother anything. I was handling this all on my own. A day or two response to a request for a meeting turned into a week. No return call. When I again called Father Brentley, he apologized for the delay and said he had some information to share. He proceeded to tell me that he spoke with Marcus and Marcus admitted to all the intimate acts over all those years. He said Marcus was remorseful and was in therapy. I remember being silent on the phone, not knowing how to respond to what I was just told. Then Father Brentley said, "Marcus admitted to being attracted to you and he admitted his attraction to his spiritual advisor years prior." Wait...what? You are telling me Marcus ADMITTED sexually molesting me years prior, and that was it? I started to respond to this information and Father Brentley quickly

interrupted, “You have to understand, Susan, Marcus is human and these things happen. And after all, he is a good priest.” Father Brentley continued, “Based on what I have heard, no serious action will be taken.” After gathering what few thoughts I had, I demanded a meeting with the Bishop. Looking back, I am damn proud of myself for insisting on a meeting, considering I was just told to fuck off. Father Brentley sounded annoyed and a bit taken aback, but said, “Fine, then. I will speak to the Bishop.” I then asked a simple question: “What did the Bishop say when you told him?” After a brief silence there was an answer, “The Bishop has not been informed.” Again...what? You have had this information for over a week, and have not told your boss that one of his priests had been a pedophile for eight years? My fear and vulnerability was turning into rage and impatience. Father Brentley ended the conversation with, “I will call you soon, please do not call back.” But then a quick clarification: “Unless of course you have information about others who may have been harmed.” So he used the word “harmed” referring to others and wanted me to play Sherlock Holmes for THEM, but stated earlier that “no serious action would be taken” for me. I remember hanging up the phone and grabbing a paper and pen. My intuition told me to write down word for word what had just transpired. I knew in my gut I would need it later. That night, I remember lying in bed pounding my fists. I must have gotten up a dozen times; pacing and cursing. I COULD NOT believe what I was told. More importantly, how I was treated. A quick flashback to a session with my therapist flooded my brain: hire an attorney. Believe it or not, I still did not want to go that route; not just yet.

> I REMEMBER HIM ASKING EXTREMELY GRAPHIC QUESTIONS. I KNEW THAT WOULD BE A PART OF IT, BUT I DID NOT EXPECT IT IN THE FIRST FIVE MINUTES

Another week comes and goes. No phone call from Father Brentley. AGAIN I called him and this time, I took control of the conversation. “Does the Bishop know?” I asked directly. “No,” Father Brentley responded, but quickly continued, “However, I am not satisfied with what is going on, and have set up a meeting with Father Simonski.” “Who the fuck is Father Simonski?” I remember thinking. And why does he have to be involved and not the Bishop? When Father Brentley asked if I would attend, I dazedly replied “yes” figuring at least it was a meeting with someone. I guess we were heading somewhere. After another week of waiting and wondering,

Father Brentley, Father Simonski and I were scheduled to meet at the Cathedral; the same Cathedral Marcus was stationed in years prior, and a place I knew very well. When I arrived, an older woman answered the door and escorted me to a small office. I remember smelling incense and getting sick to my stomach. She closed the door behind me and I waited. After a short time, Father Brentley and Father Simonski walked in and sat next to each other across from me. Two against one. Father Brentley began by explaining to Father Simonski our phone conversations and comments made by Marcus himself. Father Simonski commented with his approval that Marcus was receiving counseling. BFD. Father Simonski then uttered words I never imagined I would hear: "The Church preaches forgiveness, Susan. Marcus is a man, and men do these things. We must forgive him and help him." As God is my witness that is word for word what was said! I remember just staring at them, desperately wanting to say, "Do you really believe the shit you are shoveling my way?" I gathered my composure and asked, "What does the Bishop say about this?" Both priests looked at each other with the response of Father Brentley being, "He is still not aware." Father Simonski quickly interjected and said, "Father Brentley, I think it best the Bishop be informed as soon as possible and another meeting be arranged." Gee...ya think?!? I was told the Bishop would be told that day and another meeting be finalized by the end of the week, but after all the broken promises up until then, I was not holding my breath.

Believe it or not, I received a phone call the next day (as promised) and was told the Bishop had finally been "filled in." Father Brentley then said, "Understand, Susan, we have no intentions of moving Marcus mainly because no real sexual activity took place." He continued, "If there had been actual sexual activity, he would have been removed immediately." Now this was getting infuriating. Remember I started to tell Father Brentley details weeks ago, only to be told, "I don't need to hear intimate details." You say you want to fix this without the necessary information. How convenient. I remember then spewing graphic details in order to get his attention. And it did. After a few minutes of my divulging, Father Brentley interrupted and said, "Oh...well, this sheds new light on the matter." I was assured then that a meeting would be arranged with me and the Bishop.

I insisted the meeting be ONLY with me and the Bishop, and at first Father Brentley agreed. Before hanging up, though, he threw out a possibility: "What if we all meet together." WE meaning the Bishop,

Father Brentley, Father Simonski, Marcus and I. He then said, “If you are not comfortable with this arrangement, you can meet with Marcus and his counselor privately.” At this point, I was so angry and felt so brutalized my mouth was looser than ever. “No,” I said quietly. “And no, I do not believe my attorney would agree with that arrangement either. “Oh....OH, your attorney?” Father Brentley said. “Yes, my attorney,” I responded. “I wish to meet alone with the Bishop as soon as possible.” Father Brentley then said, “You will hear from me tomorrow.” Now remember I had not even called an attorney yet as I was waiting/hoping for a peaceful and fair resolution. Listening to the tenor of these several conversations that was not meant to be. The next day, a meeting date was set up with the Bishop, and I was asked if my attorney would be present. “No,” I said. After that, they agreed to abide by my wishes and have only the Bishop in attendance.

I again returned to the Cathedral and was greeted by the same older woman as before. I was again escorted to a small office and was left alone to wait. My heart was jumping out of my shirt as I heard voices in the hallway. The door opened and in walked two men. I recognized the Bishop because his picture was everywhere. But the other guy, not at all. And the other guy was wearing a business suit, not a collar like the priests wear. The Bishop approached me and shook my hand. He thanked me for coming. He introduced his companion as his “administrator.” When I asked what exactly that was, I was given a roundabout explanation, then finally told “the Diocesan lawyer.” Oh, so I agree not to bring my attorney (even though I didn’t have one yet) and you agree to meet with me privately, only to ambush me at the last minute. Slick and calculated. I wanted to leave so badly, but quickly decided to continue the meeting in the hopes of an end. The Bishop told me he was informed by Father Brentley and Father Simonski of my “concerns,” not my experience, and asked me to provide further details. Both men leaned forward and listened attentively as I began to explain my abuse piece by piece. When I started to go into specific detail they both became obviously uncomfortable. Their compassion and concern took an abrupt U-turn. I remember the Bishop saying, “Well, Marcus is a man, and men do these things (same thing Father Brentley said). What if we had another meeting with Marcus to discuss this further? I’m sure he would like to talk with you and straighten this all out.” Sound familiar? It’s like they all had a script they had rehearsed and were following it to the letter. Believe it or not, at this point, I actually entertained the idea of meeting with Marcus. Sounded

reasonable. Let's sit down and talk.

Suddenly something came over me and my inner voice kicked in loud and clear. It was saying, "Hell no! Don't do it!" Did he actually say, "Men do these things"? After a few quick breaths and help from my spiritual angels, I told the Bishop and his administrator that a "sit down" was unacceptable. I wanted something done, and I wanted it done soon. At first both men looked at one another and raised their eyebrows. Then the Bishop assured me, "something will be done." And that was that, meeting over. Both men shook my hand and hurried along. I called an attorney when I got home that day and met with him the day after. I could not trust this "matter" would be handled quickly, if at all. And my attorney agreed.

The next day at work, and before the meeting with my attorney, I broke down and told a teacher friend everything that was going on. I was really alone and feeling like I would soon explode. I talked and cried to my teacher friend. I remember her being so kind, and listening to my every word. When I was done purging (at least for the moment), she said she hated the fact that I was going to the attorney alone. She offered to go with me. When I told her it wasn't necessary, she insisted. To this day, I thank her for not listening to me. We arrived at the attorney's office and were quickly asked in. The attorney did not waste time. He immediately asked me to provide specific information regarding the molestation (I was getting used to it being just that...molestation). I remember him asking extremely intimate graphic questions. I knew that would be part of it, but I did not expect it in the first five minutes. He then asked who I had told. "No one," I responded. He looked up from his legal pad with a confused look. He said, "No one? Not a soul? Not even your mother, your family?" "No," I said again. "Well..." I continued, "I did say something to a friend a couple of years ago, but it was matter of fact and lacked any detail. I pretty much just said he would hug me a lot, that's all." It was important to me to be completely honest and accurate. "Well, that's disclosure," he said, as he wrote down the approximate month and year I spoke to my friend. He told me that he had a hard time believing I had not told anyone except that one friend years ago. What can I say; victims are good at keeping secrets. When he was done, he put down the pen and sat back in his chair. He took a deep breath and then explained "how this all works." He began with the ever-lovely "most lawyers do not want to touch this" because it involved the Church. Not what I wanted to hear. Many of his colleagues were Catholic. And those that weren't did not want to get "mixed up" with the Church (his exact words). I was beginning to see why. He quickly deduced that I had gone over the current statute of limitations by about one month. Evidently, my drunken confession to my friend two years prior was enough to start the statute of limitations clock ticking. I remember his words exactly: "If you would have come here a month ago, we'd be talking a million dollar law suit and criminal charges." "Ok," I said bewildered. "But the facts are still facts and what happened still happened." "Not in the eyes of the law," he explained. According to him, "the best" we could do was to sue the Diocese and hope for the best. I asked him to stop talking at that point to catch my breath. I told him I wanted and needed therapy with an experienced counselor, and I needed it now. He agreed. He informed me he would send a letter to the Diocese tomorrow with a monetary amount expressly earmarked for therapeutic intervention. He then interjected a sobering condition: I would need to sign a confidentiality agreement with the Diocese. I had no idea what that meant, so he explained. In signing this agreement, I promised to never EVER EVER discuss the specifics and agreement made with Marcus or the Diocese. NEVER. I did not like the feeling of that. I was still going through my Master's program in Counseling and was more and more aware of the healing power of disclosure. Short story, there would be none of that. I distinctly remember him saying, "You'll get a settlement, go to therapy and it will go away...you'll see. And besides," he continued, "this is the best you will get, take it or leave it." I remember asking him two things. First, was Marcus still an active priest? And second, could the Diocese pay for my therapy directly instead of me signing the agreement? At first he said he would look into each of these, but quickly retracted, "The Diocese is not going to want a paper trail. They probably won't go for paying a therapist directly." I agreed to his drafting the letter to the Diocese. I asked my friend Rose if I could use her mailing address for all correspondences because my mother still did not know anything. She agreed. We left the meeting and I again waited.

Within a couple of weeks, interoffice envelopes at school would come to me from Rose with lawyer letters. After three or four letters back and forth, an agreement was reached. I was to receive fifteen thousand dollars with three thousand going to my attorney. Twelve thousand dollars to absolve eight years of chronic sadistic abuse (not to mention being pimped out) with no admission of fault by the Church or Marcus. A lot to process. I remember getting that second to last letter stating the agreement details. They were buying my silence. But when I brought that up with my attorney, he chose to put a different spin on it."Susan," he said, "You don't want to talk about this forever anyway. Go to therapy. It will get better, you'll see." The day came for me to return to the attorney and sign the confidentiality agreement, otherwise known as a lifelong secrecy pact. I went alone this time. My attorney read through the agreement and emphasized the need for confidentiality. When he was through, I asked if he had answers to my questions about Marcus and therapy. He did. He said the Diocese said Marcus was "not in charge of any church" and that he was "sent away for extensive therapy." When I pressed further, my attorney seemed annoyed and looked up at the clock. I stopped asking questions. Staring down at this piece of paper, I had this huge knot in my stomach. My gut was saying, "DON'T SIGN THIS. "What choice did I have? I needed therapy, I needed the money, and they knew it. With pen in hand, my attorney uttered these profound words: "Once you sign this, it's like it never happened." I remember thinking that maybe signing this would make things go away; a huge rationalization at a very pivotal moment. After signing, he told me I would receive my copy of the agreement along with a check (after his expenses) in a couple of weeks. He also said these penetrating words: "You know, they didn't even want to give you this much. They see you as a gold digger." Why he chose to tell me that I will never know. I felt this money was for services rendered. Instead of being happy about the settlement, I left his office feeling cheap, guilty and depressed. I never heard back from the Church like they said I would after the meeting with the Bishop and his "administrator." Maybe it was punishment for my legal action against them. Maybe my "gold digging" was offensive and UN-Christian. I was forbidden to contact ANYONE in the Church as per the confidentiality agreement. Pretty ironclad. And very done.

CHAPTER NINE

BE NOT AFRAID...WELL, MAYBE A LITTLE AFRAID...

"Act like it never happened." That was my mantra the next several years. Even though I knew I needed therapy again, I was not willing to dredge things up. I put therapy on the back burner. I kept myself busy with teaching and graduate school. I moved out of Mom's house to my first apartment. I was dating a woman and soon we moved in together. I graduated with my Master's Degree in Counselor Education and got a job as a School Counselor. Things were moving ahead. I really thought things were good. Still, my anxiety and depression were at an all-time high as well as my drinking. I was having nightmares and haunting vivid memories. If I got three or four hours sleep a night, it was a good night. Acting like it never happened was not working. Mom was worried. I told her my feelings were about my father (she still didn't know anything about Marcus or the church meetings or the confidentiality agreement). She suggested therapy and she was right. Reluctantly, I found another therapist and began weekly sessions. On top of my own issues, as a Counselor, I was now working with dozens of people each week who were experiencing anxiety, depression, loss and grief. It was a lot to take in. My new therapist (like my former therapist) cut to the chase pretty quickly and validated my abusive past. When I brought the confidentiality agreement to a session one day, her mouth hung open. I had told her about it prior, but somehow seeing it must have shocked her. I remember her reading it shaking her head. I remember her glancing up at me from time to time looking for some reaction. There was none. I mean, come on...what was there to do? I signed this document stating I would NEVER EVER talk about ANY of this to ANYONE for the rest of my life. My lawyer made that clear to me. Besides, my Graduate program gave me all the tools I needed to work through my abuse on my own and to let it go forever (amazing how we can rationalize!).

As therapy continued, it became crystal clear that the secrets I was keeping were holding me back and preventing me from truly, "moving forward." I needed to reach out with my story and hopefully connect with other victims. But before I did that, I needed to tell my family. I remember telling my

brother and sister first. They were my testing ground for telling my mother. I remember telling them separately and both being kind and listening attentively. They were confused at times with certain content, but overall they gave me exactly what I needed: support. They were angry and sad, but incredibly supportive. I am lucky for that. Then I told my mother. I will never forget sitting in her TV room in my father's old recliner. I told her I needed to say something, but I kept stopping. At first, she was patient, but began getting annoyed. So I blurted it out: "Father Marcus abused me." I remember her looking at me for a couple of seconds, staring at me actually. "What?" she said. I repeated the phrase. "What do you mean abused?" she asked once, then twice, then more. To say she was less than understanding is an understatement. She let me talk for a few minutes, and then began a barrage of questions and comments. "Is that why you...?" was a question I heard over and over. I remember stopping her, saying, "Mom, I know this is a lot to take in." She was silent. Her incessant talking fell silent. She was emotionless. At some point she left the room. No hug, no encouraging words, nothing. I was alone. After what seemed to be an eternity, she came back and again began the inquisition. Most times my answer was "yes" or "I didn't know it was wrong." I vividly remember her retort: "How could you NOT KNOW it was wrong?" Her eyes were wide and angry. Her voice shaking and shrill. Every single comment was blaming me, not blaming him. I wish my therapist would have prepared me for her reaction. As I came to find out later, this type of reaction was fairly common with parents of abuse survivors. I know now she never blamed me. She was rationally processing the fact that her baby girl had been repeatedly violated...and under her watch. Neither one of us spoke about "it" again right away. As the days and weeks went by, Mom started softening. She started asking more questions and started sharing her thoughts and feelings. I told her about the meeting I had with the Bishop and the several conversations with the other priests. I also told her about the lawyer and the confidentiality agreement. Looking back, she was amazing. She took in so much and chipped away asking questions. Mom was not accusatory as she had been. Instead she was helpful and supportive; growing more and more angry at Marcus. I remember her saying, "Wait a minute, didn't he come to your eighth grade graduation party?" "Yes," I said. "He sat in my backyard and ate my food while that was going on? "Yes," I said. "Didn't he sit there drinking with your father?" "Yep," I said again. The term in therapy is "processing" and believe me, she was processing. She was getting it big time.

My girlfriend and I broke up several months later. Although Mom was pretty okay with me being gay, she later admitted not liking "that one" at all. So my breakup was a good thing, for her and for me. I asked Mom if I could move back home with her for a while to sort things out. There was no hesitation at all. Mom said, "of course, honey, come home." That made up for all the judgment she initially threw at me when I told her about Marcus. She was so welcoming and warm. I was back in my old room as an adult in my thirties. Weird, wonderful, crazy...all at the same time! We talked and acted like adults. I was discovering things about Mom I never knew and actually enjoyed spending time with her. Even though we didn't talk a lot about Marcus, she let me share whatever I needed to. Occasionally she would ask a question or need clarification. And I would answer honestly each time. She could not handle graphic details (which was fine). Just her asking was incredibly validating. She started telling me how proud she was of me for telling the Bishop and "standing up for myself." That felt good. After about three months, I found a nice apartment close to the beach and lived there until I bought my first home. Mom gave me a generous down payment and helped me maneuver the mortgage mumbo jumbo. Along with my Aunt Reggie, she also went door-to-door in my new townhouse community asking people if they liked living there! I remember being embarrassed at first, but as I write this now, I realize she loved me more then I knew. Right now, I am wiping away tears of gratitude!

My first home on my own. It was early 2000. I was tenured in a new school district (I had become older and wiser to the game-playing in the work world). I was going out a lot dancing and partying. New beginnings, new hope, new life. There was one club in particular that was my favorite, until I saw Marcus there. Yep, as I was coming out of the bathroom and walking down the hallway, he was walking towards me. I hadn't seen him in years. He was heavier and balder, but it was him. I will never forget his happy greeting, "Susan, hi, how are you?" I walked past him and fell right into a panic attack. I remember leaving the bar quickly and walking up to the boardwalk along the ocean. I was hyperventilating and shaking. One of my friends followed me out and asked what was going

> I REMEMBER HER SAYING "WAIT A MINUTE, DIDN'T HE COME TO YOUR EIGHTH GRADE PARTY?" "YES, I SAID". HE SAT IN MY BACKYARD AND ATE MY FOOD WHILE THAT WAS GOING ON?" "YES" I SAID

on. I did not want to go into details, so she got the cliff notes version. "Do you want to leave?" I remember her asking. "Yes, no, yes, no." I went back and forth for several minutes. Finally, I gathered the courage to go back inside and rejoin my friends. I had to walk right past Marcus and his entourage (mostly younger males). My friend who had been outside with me saw him and immediately walked over and started yelling in his face. I heard her call him a scum bag and a coward. So cool. Marcus quickly motioned to one of his boys to get up and handle the situation. The young man got in front of my friend and started pushing her away. Marcus sat there glaring at her, then at me. After a minute or so more, Kat (my friend) walked away and rejoined our group. Of all the quintessential moments in my life, that is by far one of my favorite. Someone FINALLY stood up to him! And she thought enough of me to do it. We stayed a bit longer that night, but then I had to leave. I had enough. I remember getting home around midnight and calling Mom in a panic. She was great. She listened and tried calming me down. There really wasn't anything to say. But the fact that she let me talk and cry was a blessing. I stayed away from the bars for a while out of pure fear. I drank at home and entertained there too. I justified it as a needed "break from the scene." but when you really boil it down, he still had control over me. I had to do something. The fear and secrecy was killing me. It was time for a family meeting.

My brother, sister and mother knew all about Marcus and the attorney letters and meetings and confidentiality agreement. They knew the facts. What they did not know was the ongoing emotional turmoil I was going through. And with the Boston Church scandal still alive in the news, they needed to know. We met at Mom's house one weekend day and sat in her TV room. One by one, we shared our thoughts and feeling about what was going on in Boston, as well as in our own family. I told them I wanted another meeting with the Bishop; this time, with my family there. The purpose of the meeting was to release me from the Confidentiality Agreement I had signed twelve years earlier. As my brother and sister can be over-analytical, I had to explain what this agreement had done to me over the years, and how stifled and suffocated I felt. I remember them listening and trying to understand. My sister seemed unnerved by the conversation, and several times interrupted me, interjecting her own thoughts. I used my handy-dandy counseling skills and redirected the conversation; clarifying when necessary. The bottom line was I needed their support. Mom mostly listened, but when she did speak she was one hundred percent in favor of a meeting. She knew I would go with or without them and, as she put it, "You are NOT going alone this time." My brother was the next to jump on board. Looking back, I don't think he completely agreed with my rationale for such a meeting, but he was supportive all the same. My sister was the last holdout. I don't know if it was anger at the Church, or Marcus, or me. She was difficult. When it came time to set a date, Mom and my brother said exactly what I needed to hear: "Anytime." I remember my brother saying, "You tell me when, Sue, and I will be there." Mom joked at that point and said, "I'm retired, so my calendar is pretty much open!" We needed that comic relief. My sister hemmed and hawed. As a college professor, I tried to be understanding about her teaching schedule. The reality was, I worked too, and so did my brother. She gave me a list of days that were not good. When I explained that the Bishop may only give me one or two choices, I remember her saying, "Well, ask for more." Seriously! I started getting a little impatient and heated, so my brother interjected. He calmly looked at my sister and said, "We need to do this for Sue." She did not appear overly moved, but agreed to be as flexible as possible. I called the Diocese the next day and again jumped through some royal hoops attempting to set up a meeting. At first, the priest I spoke to claimed to have no knowledge of any agreement with Marcus. And a meeting with the Bishop could take months. "Not acceptable," I remember saying calmly to Father Whoever. "My family and I expect a meeting to be set up soon." Man I had some brass balls looking back! But you know what? At that point, I was not going to be bullied, or talked down to, or intimidated by ANYONE. Someone must have known something, because within a couple of days, I was given several options. Mom: "Of course, Susan, any day." My brother: "Tell me when and I will be there." My sister: "No, no and I have to see." I was infuriated. Whatever her reason or motivation, she was making this about her, and I would not have it. It almost came down to a screaming match over the phone one night, until finally she agreed on a day and time. Looking back, her reactions were similar to Mom. She was angry at them and initially directing it at me. I called the Bishop's office the next day and confirmed a meeting within the next two weeks. I expressly requested ONLY my family and the Bishop be present, and was told my request would be honored. Just us. No one else. We were set.

The day before the meeting, I called my family to confirm (which was probably the third or fourth time I reminded them). We agreed to meet at Mom's house and all drive together. I got to Mom's early that morning and she was dressed and ready (bless her heart). My brother arrived shortly after and we sat in the TV room waiting for my sister. The clock was ticking and she still was not there. She did have a habit of being late, but that habit was tearing at my insides. I remember pacing and cursing. Mom was so great trying to calm me down. With minutes to spare, my sister arrived. I didn't want to hear explanations or apologies; I just wanted to go. I remember feeling like I had a team, a spiritual posse who believed in me and wanted to fight for me. I was going to finally get the "mea culpa" I longed for all those years. When we drove into the parking lot, I remember asking my family for a minute alone. I stood by the car and closed my eyes and prayed. I still believed in God, and I asked God (and Dad) for guidance and a peaceful resolution. After I finished praying, I set my cell phone on record. God was great, but modern technology could come in handy depending on the content of the meeting. I had been through a lot with "these people" and was not going to be messed with! I took a deep breath, and in we went. We were escorted to a large meeting room and offered water. We were told the Bishop would be right with us. Soon the door opened and in walked the Bishop...along with another man; a sharply dressed smiling man. Both the Bishop and "this man" made their way around the room shaking our hands and asked us to be seated. I immediately asked who this man was and why he was there. I was told by the Bishop "not to worry" and that he was simply an "overseer"of the Diocese. The Bishop immediately began with apologies: "I am truly sorry for the actions of Father Marcus. Please accept my deepest apologies." I quickly looked back at the "overseer" and again asked for clarification as to who he was. Again, I was told he was an "overseer." My brother looked at me concerned and my sister looked at this guy as if to say "who the fuck are you?" "We are all on your side, Susan," I remember the Bishop saying as he looked into my eyes. "We care about your welfare and the welfare of your family. We are here for you." I took a deep breath and reluctantly continued the meeting.

My mother was the first to speak for our family. I could cry now when I think about it. She told the Bishop and his "overseer" how she entrusted me to the church as a young girl. How the CYO was supposed to be a safe place. And how betrayed she felt when she found out what Marcus had done, over and over. The Bishop and his "overseer" listened to her every word, both leaning forward. My sister described how hard it was for her to hear what had happened. She said no family should have to hear their daughter or sister say they were molested, especially by a priest. The Bishop and his home boy agreed. Then I spoke, sometimes through tears, explaining the sheer hell I was living and how upsetting it was that this was allowed to happen for so long. My brother was the last. He explained how this confidentiality agreement (which my family each had a copy of) was strangling me, like an albatross around my neck. I didn't know what the word albatross meant, but I looked it up when I got home. My brother insisted this agreement needed to be nullified in order for me to truly heal. It's important to mention that we did not rehearse anything that was said that day. We all spoke from our hearts. I am proud of that. After my brother finished, the tone of the meeting changed dramatically and two interesting things happened next.

First, the Bishop spoke and claimed to have no knowledge of the agreement, or any misconduct by Marcus for that matter. He CLAIMED that this day was "the first he had heard of it." I remember us looking at each other and at the Bishop in amazement. How on earth could the leader of this Diocese not know? He had replaced the previous Bishop and was newer to the job, I'll give him that. I believed (and still believe) they did know about Marcus. Second, the "overseer" suddenly became agitated and loud. Keep in mind, up until that point; he was smiling, acknowledging...even expressing sadness over what had transpired with Marcus. But as soon as my brother requested the agreement be absolved, he flipped a switch. I remember him leaning forward addressing my brother, finger pointed, and saying, "Now wait just a minute! So what do you want...what do you REALLY want?" My family and I were shocked. I remember my mother giving him a look which I knew well. That look meant, "Do not speak to me like that!" Voices began to rise. My brother (usually a soft-spoken guy) started challenging the "overseer." It was getting weird. At that point, the Bishop leaned toward the "overseer" and put his hand on his arm as if to say, "Calm down." I looked at the Bishop, and pointing at the "overseer," asked one more time, "What does this man do here?" "He is the Diocesan Administrator," the Bishop said. "Oh, so he is your lawyer," I said. I remember my mother shooting me a look as if to say, "Susan, you shouldn't have said that." After a brief pause and a glance toward the "overseer," the Bishop said, "Yes, he is our attorney." So Mr. Overseer, now better known as Mr. Lawyer, began spewing "legalese"; confirming my suspicions all along. They were not there for ME, and they could not care less about MY WELFARE. Their sole purpose was to protect the church. I sat back in my chair in complete disgust. My mother expressed anger and resentment to the Bishop for

being lied to. My sister chimed in too. She was NOT happy we were told this would be a private meeting. The Bishop redirected, or at least tried to. More exchanges happened. I gotta give my family credit. That day, they were on fire. The administrator/lawyer then interjected, saying we needed to end the meeting. The Bishop told us he needed time "to process" what was discussed, and would get back to us soon with his decision. He apologized at the end, as he did in the beginning, for what had taken place with Marcus. But remember he said he had to acknowledge that it took place. So why the apology? The attorney caught on and abruptly shook all our hands and left the room. We were left in that room alone, shaking our heads. I remember walking back to the car to finish my bottle of iced tea. I wanted to smash it.

One month came and went. I called the Bishop's office. No return call. I wrote him a letter and mailed it certified. Two months, then three. Mom called the Bishop this time. No return call. After four months of waiting and wondering, an answer came. The Bishop would not nullify the confidentiality agreement because it would be "irresponsible" for him to do so. So instead of this agreement going up in smoke, I was told it would forever exist. The Bishop, however, did say I was free to discuss what happened with Marcus to anyone; I just could not discuss the financial arrangement. But then he wrote that if I did discuss the financial arrangement, he "would not take action against me." Gee whiz, how sweet! So for almost ten years I was told I COULD NOT discuss anything, and now you were saying I could. At least it was something.

Chapter Ten
I WILL NEVER LEAVE YOU OR FORSAKE YOU...

After the family meeting with the Bishop, my therapist and I discussed making a list of old CYO friends and "rectory rats." She explained how part of my healing was confronting the abuser (or in this case, the institution who allowed the abuse) and part was reaching out to others. She assured me that it would ultimately be the best thing. I was not so sure. I remember having conflicting thoughts. Some were about the joy of connecting with another Marcus survivor. Others were about the sadness and anger that he did this to another person. Even jealousy entered in. Would I feel jealous if someone else was one of his "special friends?" We had to wait and see. Before the days of Google, I searched through phone books and found friends and friends of friends; I assembled a list of names, addresses and phone numbers. My therapist and I were working on journaling, so we decided it was best to write letters instead of calling. I also decided to write a letter to each parish Marcus was in and notify the acting pastor. Remember the brothers from that last party with Marcus? I found them too and drafted a heartfelt and concerned letter. I did it for myself, but also for them. I really wanted to save them from years of torment. Even though the Bishop gave his written word I was free to discuss publicly what I needed, I was skeptical and guarded. I wrote each letter anonymously; no signature or return address. Well, except for one; the letter to the brothers. I wanted them and their families to know how to find me if they needed help. That's what I was all about; helping people. I remember the day I mailed this stack of letters feeling joyful and powerful. I was SO happy and SO sure this would be a good thing.

About a month later, I got a large inner-office envelope at work from Rose (my teacher friend who went with me to the first lawyer meeting). What was in that envelope still shocks me to this day. It was a letter from my attorney and a copy of a letter from another attorney. My attorney's letter stated there was "reasonable proof" I had violated the confidentiality agreement I signed years prior. The other attorney's letter stated he had received a signed letter from me that was "grossly defamatory" to his client (that would be Marcus) and to his reputation. One of the brothers was still in contact with Marcus and gave Marcus the letter I sent him. I started to shake and hyperventilate. I felt faint. I needed to leave. I had another teacher call the principal, and I bolted. I sat in my car for a few minutes reading and re-reading these letters, completely overwhelmed. My ABUSER had the right to prosecute ME if I did not cease and desist. My abuser had the upper hand. I got home and immediately phoned my attorney. He was annoyed and condescending. "Susan," I remember him saying, "You KNEW you could not talk about this to ANYONE. WHY did you do this?" Sounded like Mom. I was dumbfounded listening on the other end. He went on and on about not making my life or his any harder. I had to cease and desist. Fuck this life!

The next day, I called out of work and was alone. I drank and ate and drove and drank some more. By late afternoon, I was pretty tanked. And much to my embarrassment and shame, I chose to drive drunk. I drove aimlessly up and down the local highways, then headed for the shore. I needed more booze so I stopped somewhere and got a fifth of whiskey. I drove and cried and yelled and drank. After everything that I had gone through, this was worse than all the feel-ups and erections and orgasms. I wanted to die. According to these letters, Marcus could charge me with violating his rights. Oh, and the fact that the Church viewed me as a gold digger was enough to seal the deal. I vaguely remember speeding up next to a truck and then to the highway divider. By the grace of God (and Dad riding shotgun) I somehow made it home that night and back into my townhouse. I woke up the next morning fully clothed and sicker than I had ever been. I fumbled around for the phone and called into work. Another sick day. I spent that morning throwing up, crying and cursing. I guess I really didn't want to die, because if I did, it would have happened. I remember staring at a picture of Dad sobbing and pleading. I can't tell you exactly what happened, but it was then that I knew I never wanted to die again. I needed to work through this and get whatever control I could. I called Mom.

I arrived to her house with the letters in hand. She could tell I was physically unwell. She sat on her couch and read through the letters. I could tell she was confused and angry. We talked about how the Bishop had "given his permission" for me to talk about this. And that's all I was doing. I remember us shaking our heads and looking down. When she did look at me, her eyes were watery and sad. She admitted the day I first told her about Marcus she was never angry

I WANTED TO DIE

at me and in the time that had passed she put things into perspective. She also shared how angry she was that Dad was dead, because if he wasn't she would, and I quote: "have him kick the shit out of Marcus." She admitted her initial reaction was bad and asked for my forgiveness. That was a gift I will always cherish. I remember hugging and crying. She looked at me in the eyes and said, "We WILL get through this." In a crazy cosmic way, all of this brought Mom and I closer and we remained that way for the rest of her life. She told me more and more how proud she was that I had endured so much and how grateful she was to have me for a daughter. By contrast, she shared how helpless she felt and how angry she was becoming. They were hard talks, but great talks.

I wanted and needed vindication. And the vindication came. Our local newspapers were suddenly publishing the names of priests accused of sexual abuse. It seemed dozens of young adults were coming forward in droves. I remember picking up the paper one morning and freezing when I saw Marcus' name right there in print! Now this did not mean he was guilty, of course. But it did mean that at least one other person accused him of sex crimes. I was not traumatized or thrown into a depression or rage. I can honestly tell you I felt...well...good. I was never a gold digger like the Diocese said, and I was never crazy. I was a victim. In reading further, the article said to contact the local sex crimes division of our town if we had information on these priests. I remember Mom wishing I would drop the whole thing and asking me not to proceed. She was worried I might spiral. But after thinking about it and again praying on it, I decided to give them a call. I was not ready to put it down just yet. An appointment was set up quickly for an interview. Although my abuse happened well over a decade prior, they were still interested in talking with me. How validating that someone actually wanted to talk with, and listen to ME! I remember the day they came to my home, one male and one female investigator. Very, very nice people. At the dining room table, I showed them letters and pictures, and gave them the chronology of events. I remember the female seeming empathetic, smiling as if to telepathically say, "This sucks!" After over an hour, they politely explained they would keep my testimony on file; however there was nothing else that could be done. You know what...I decided to take that as a good thing. For nothing else, it was documented by a government agency. Forever. Between speaking with the Sex Crimes Unit and seeing Marcus' name in print, I finally got the true validation I had hoped for.

Mom was always good at looking at the positive. Not that any of this

WAS positive. She encouraged me to put all this down and remain focused on the good; to embrace my life and feel grateful for what I had. I admit I was pissed at her then for stressing the positive because I interpreted that as downplaying or even dismissing what had happened to me. It was quite the contrary. Mom was teaching me that even though we could not erase the past, we did have control over the present and future. It was over. And it was up to me to live my life in my way. Ironically, Mom taught me a lot about the Law of Attraction without either one of us knowing it! So we agreed to move ahead, really ahead this time. But you know the old saying: "it isn't over til it's over".

Chapter Eleven
GOD HELPS THOSE WHO HELP THEMSELVES...

"Move on." It was my mantra. It was Mom's mantra. It was a good thing. And for a short time, I cushioned myself from news about abusive priests and stopped journal-writing and therapy. I really WANTED to be done. But as much as my mind was saying to put it all down, my intuition chimed in with "not just yet." There was one more go-round to go round.

I heard of an organization called SNAP which was specifically for survivors of clergy abuse. I found them online and began reading through dozens of accounts of abuse from both men and women. You could specifically search for a person or city to get information from other survivors. I found posts about Marcus and about Bishops in my county and state. It was illuminating. It was enlightening, astonishing, exhausting. I suddenly had a team of thousands! What was most interesting were the posts from survivors of not just priests from my Diocese, but Bishops as well. To say the Bishop we met with had no idea of past events was, in my opinion, an out-and-out lie. In my opinion, many clergy on every level were involved in some way. Like the priest that was Marcus' confessor. Why didn't he tell? Or maybe he did, but was told that the sanctity of confession far outweighed the protection of children. How on earth was it humanly possible that so many knew and no one acted?

My euphoria of having a team of thousands changed to utter depression and anger. Not ONE person cared enough to act? Not one? I know, for instance, that other priests in the rectory saw Marcus with young people in his room. I saw them witness this time and time again. I believe the word is "bystander." So, so, so many bystanders. That was one piece my mother finally came to grips with. She went from originally proclaiming "one or two bad apples" to "oh my God, there are so many who knew." Yes, Mom, they did.

I began sending my family information and posts from SNAP. They were pleasantly polite, but hardly ever responded. I would press the send button hoping and expecting a barrage of support and disgust. Nothing. Mom, my brother and sister said nothing, Looking back, I'm sure it was a struggle for them to read what I sent and wish to remain Catholic.

It still was their Church (as my sister once said). I admit to being enraged for not feeling their support like I had felt the day of the Bishop meeting. My father's saying: "pissing in the wind" seemed to fit. I wanted them to see the realities of it all. Maybe they did, but did not know how to handle it. Growing up in any religion is an interesting thing; our parents tell us what to believe. There was no option. And even as adults we tend to continue with childhood indoctrination whether we truly want to or not. In any case, I know my family struggled reading so much about a church they believed in.

Around this time I got an unexpected phone call from the Bishop's office. It was another "administrator." He explained how he knew about my meeting with the Bishop years before and that they were considering releasing me from the confidentiality agreement. I was intrigued but very skeptical. All of a sudden, these guys want to help me? He continued. He explained how they wanted to laicize Marcus (take away his priestly title). But in order to do that, they needed my help. Now you would think I'd have jumped at the chance to spill my guts...AGAIN. After all, this albatross could once and for all be removed from my neck. But some- thing inside me said "no." I asked the "administrator" if they were ready to terminate the agreement even if I did not help them. A quick and emphatic "no." That was that. Yet again, you are leveraging for your own benefit, I remember thinking. I told him to remove the agreement first, and then I would be happy to tell them what I knew. I never heard back from him. I had had enough. It was back to "move on"...period. I branched out of my school-based counseling and began working part-time at a group practice. It was my first job as a therapist, not a counselor. I didn't have a clue what I was doing, but like any job, you learn. One of the therapists on staff was so sweet and nurturing. She had been there for several years and had over a decade of experience. She was also very insightful...and very gay. A friend at the time thought this was great for me. She reminded me of how many relationships I had in the past and how a friend was just what I needed. And Kate became that friend. Besides, I was not interested in her at all. She had terribly short hair, dressed on the "butch" side, and smoked. No way. She would be a friend, period. As weeks and months went by, we would talk out of the office and occasionally get together. She was so quiet! But maybe that's what I needed at the time; to drown out all the chaos and chatter with silence. As much as I liked working in group practice, the strain of two jobs was too much. I left within a year.

Kate and I kept in touch and became closer friends. I started to open up more about my past relationships and about Marcus. I remember her being so in tune; listening to every word. Something about her made me feel like everything I was saying was okay. It was the first time I had told anyone that much about Marcus; not even my longest and closest friends. One day, I was in my living room and Kate pulled up. When she got out of her car, I saw her carrying a yellow rose. My heart started racing. I remember thinking,"Uhh...why is she bringing me a flower? And a rose no less?" I didn't want to let her in. I was pacing and panicking. (I am laughing now as I write this how worked up I got!) I opened the door and she walked in with a big smile and my rose. She told me yellow roses mean friendship and how grateful she was that we were friends. Now I was suspicious. OK...nice gesture, and yes, yellow roses signify friendship, but something wasn't quite right. She stayed briefly, kissed me on the cheek and left. "OH SHIT" was my prominent thought!

I called a friend and asked for her interpretation. Consensus: she wanted more. But the question I had was: is that what I wanted? I was NOT good at relationships (big shocker as an abuse victim) and did not want to ruin a good friendship. I decided to play it cool and see what the future had planned.

The John Lennon song lyric, "Life is what happens while you're busy making other plans" became my reality. I was bound and determined to be Kate's friend, and only her friend, until one summer evening. I went to her apartment for drinks and dinner; no big deal; I had been there many times before. When I pulled up, she was sitting on her balcony playing her guitar and singing. She answered the door in a black tank top and shorts. Oh, Nellie! I mixed us drinks and we sat outside on the balcony exchanging light banter. She then picked up the guitar and started singing the Melissa Etheridge song, "I Wanna Come Over." Let's just say at that moment our friendship expanded! We spent the night and most of the next day together. We talked, laughed, made love. There was a comfort I felt with Kate that was new. And I liked it. She knew all about my family, my father and Marcus. AND she wanted to be with me. We decided to play it "casual." We were not IN a relationship. We were just friends with benefits. We could do this. About a week later, we went to the beach with Kate's longtime friends. I remember it being a beautiful sunny day. Karen and Diane were funny and warm and welcoming. I liked them

KATE LOVED ME, AND I FELT THE SAME

immediately. When Karen asked Kate if her "girlfriend" wanted something to drink, there was a sudden silence. It was as if everything stopped. I remember Karen making this wincing look on her face, like "Oh crap, did I say something wrong?" But she didn't say anything wrong. When Kate and I got back to her apartment that day, we talked about Karen's comment and about what we really wanted. Turns out we were both protecting ourselves from the realities of a relationship. Truth was we both wanted more. We were girlfriends, and we were in this for the long haul. Soon after that, I met Kate's longtime friends, Lorraine, Marie and Janice, and Kate's family.

Kate had (and still has) a fascinating view of healthy relationships which I still share with clients to this day: the four seasons rule. She believed that it was healthy to be with someone for all four seasons before you make a stronger commitment. A person may act and feel completely different in the summer as opposed to the winter. Better know that early on before walking down the aisle! We agreed to give it a year and walk through the four seasons together. The summer ended and fall began. Kate was turning fifty and wanted to have a big blowout, and I (of course) was on board to help. We were only together a couple of months, but I felt quite comfortable with the planning. We looked at several places at the shore, and she decided on one right on the beach. The manager told us it was off-season, so he could accommodate us. We met with a caterer and sent out invitations. It was all set. All set...that is, until a week before the party. Out of nowhere, the manager of the beach bar called Kate with news. I remember it clearly. It was a Saturday night. Kate started the conversation with a smile which quickly turned to tears. I heard her say, "Wait...what?" and "So there's nothing we can do?" When she hung up the phone, she could barely speak. "The beach bar closed...I guess I'm not having a party." I remember sitting in disbelief. I was livid. She went on to say how the manager was very sorry and wanted to help us in any way he could. Luckily, we did not give him a deposit, so that piece was a non-issue. She sobbed and shook her head. I hadn't realized just how important this party was to Kate until then. "Ok, so listen," I said, "we will make this happen." She was despondent. The next day I was up early (as I usually was and still am) and began surfing the internet for local beach restaurants and bars. I started making a list. When she got up I showed her my ideas. As she was still very upset, she was less than optimistic. I was planning a party and she was planning how to tell sixty people there WAS no party. It was our first taste of how we deal with a crisis. As always, I picked myself up and plowed ahead. This party was going to happen.

After several stressful days, we found a hotel with an available room (and it was overlooking the ocean!). Sweet! We called the caterer, the DJ and as many people as we could. It was two days before the party. We figured we could print up flyers and put them up where the party was SUPPOSED to be to direct guests to the new venue (which by the way was right across the street). The Universe works when we let it! The day of the party was a huge blur, and with very little sleep, we hung up flyers and fielded numerous phone calls. Kate's family came in from Connecticut and were extremely helpful, not just for the logistical part, but with keeping Kate from having a meltdown. With only a few minor glitches, Kate's fiftieth birthday was in progress. We began greeting guests and I began memorizing dozens of names. These were people she had known most of her life, and I was only on the scene for two months! I remember catching some eyes looking me over. It was more nerve-wracking than I thought it would be. I got through the initial introductions and scampered around like I always did at parties, making sure everyone was taken care of. Kate was having a ball drinking and dancing. She looked beautiful. When she stood up to thank every- one for coming she shared her deep thoughts about the day. "I remember telling my friends that on my fiftieth birthday, I want to be in love. And I am. Thank you Susan for being in my life." It was so heartfelt and genuine, and very unexpected. Kate loved me, and I felt the same. It was an exhausting day (especially when Kate wanted to open her presents at 2 am) but it was the first of many challenges we faced together.

We knew we wanted to buy a home together and began looking in several shore towns. Every weekend, along with coffee and breakfast sandwiches, we scoped out homes and townhomes for sale. It was an exciting time. I put my townhouse up for sale and began fielding offers. I thought I was good. We also got into the shore nightlife and went out dancing at the local gay bars. One afternoon at a Tea Dance (that's gay for afternoon dance), I saw someone I did not want to see. Marcus was standing on the top floor of an outdoor deck. He was looking down directly at me. Kate saw my demeanor changed and asked me what was wrong. At first I said nothing, but then I started to shake. She again asked what was wrong, and I pointed up to Marcus. She paused and looked up. She started walking to the staircase to get up to the second floor. I grabbed her arm, and pulled her back. She started shouting at him and pointing at him. I put my hands on her face and assured her it was okay.

But it wasn't. It took everything I had not to have a full-blown panic attack on the dance floor. We stayed a little bit longer until I asked her to leave. It killed me that my good time was ruined by him. On the ride to her apartment, we talked and processed what had happened. I again started to shake and became short of breath. We sat on her balcony and after several minutes, I came back down. That day, I decided to find out where Marcus was living. I was not going to buy a house if he was close by. The internet produced results and I had what I needed; in more ways than one.

The good news was while surfing the web we found a home in the town we liked. A seashore colonial with a picket fence on a tree-lined street. It was in our price range and seemed perfect. The not-so-good news was that while surfing the web I found out Marcus lived in that same town. You cannot make this stuff up! Kate was quick to suggest we look elsewhere. After a few days of back and forth, we decided to at least look at the house. Maybe we would hate it and that would be that. Maybe things would take care of themselves. I remember driving up to the house for the first time and standing outside. Kate and I commented on the architecture and style. As fate would have it (yet again, fate stepped in) the owner was home and invited us in. We wandered around the first floor, then the second floor, as the owner pointed out every nuance. He was so sweet and patient that night. We spent about a half hour, then left to go to my townhouse. We did not say a word until we got to my place. I know you don't know me, but you gotta understand what an accomplishment not talking was for me! I wanted Kate to share her thoughts without influencing them with mine. After two drinks were poured and a brief sit on the couch, I asked, "So, what do you think?" "I love it," she replied. Her eyebrows were raised and her smile was soft and sincere. That was our home. A realtor friend got the ball in motion and prepared the initial paperwork. We were excited and nervous and scared. By this time, we were pre-approved and my townhome had a serious buyer. It was good. But as the days went on, I thought about Marcus and had more panic attacks. I had them at work, at home, in the shower. I didn't tell Kate how bad it got. I kept wondering if I could buy a home less than a mile from where he lived. I even did several "drive-bys" to make sure he lived where the internet said. He did. Our realtor friend called us within two weeks and said our offer was accepted. Anyone who has bought a home knows it is the best and worst time of your life. I closed on my townhouse the day before we closed on our home. Much to our attorney's chagrin, we

had already moved furniture and other belongings to our new home with the owner's permission. The night before our big move, Kate stayed in her apartment and me in my townhouse one last time. I slept on the floor and had the bare necessities. I was up all night pacing and wondering, "What the hell did I just do?" The next day's move in went as planned. My only immediate need was to put up a stockade fence. I told Kate I needed to feel safe, and she understood why. We quarreled about where to put the glasses in the cabinet (right or left side) and disagreed on certain colors for rooms and bedding. Typical couples stuff. It really felt like home. I remember waking up one night and going downstairs by the fireplace. I lit a candle and then a fire. "You got this" I remember saying to myself. My dog and our cats were all gathered around, like a spiritual tribe. It was good.

Soon I realized how not good it was. We saw Marcus again on the boardwalk and once more at a bar hosting a local charity event. Each time, I lost it. I shook and sweated and cried. I could barely breathe. And each time, Kate put her arm around me and helped me through. Looking back, it must have been hard for her. What do you say, really? She could not make any of this go away. I had to do that. And I thought I was doing that. But as the months and years went by, things were getting worse again, not better. I tried talking to Mom, but by then I think she dealt with Marcus by putting it in the past, for good. She would listen when I talked, but would then change the subject quickly. Again, what do you say? As a mother, it must have ripped down to her core to have endured this journey with me. Kate and I started fighting more, and innocent quarrels turned into a strong question about us being together (at least from my end). And to top it off, Marcus started driving past our house each morning. I should mention that I tried, over the years, to call the Diocese for information on Marcus and had friends call as well. Each time when we got to saying his name, we were hung up on and told not to call back. Hence, the internet. His name was listed on a local hospital's website as an employee.

Kate was having a hard time with my meltdowns. From a completely rational perspective, I understand why. Marcus was in my past, and he had no hold on me anymore. That was logical. As a therapist, Kate had occasionally worked with abuse survivors, but this was the first time she heard consistent, in-depth accounts and saw consistent reactions. There was nothing she could do but hold me and tell me it was okay. It was wearing thin on both of us. Just when I would be "pretty okay," fate would put Marcus in front of me again and again, as if to say, "you THINK you're okay, but you're not." My therapy at that time was work. I was now a Guidance Counselor in a small working-class school district with close to three years in. I loved the helping aspect and connecting with my students. I saw myself there until retirement. I remember the day before an important school board meeting asking my principal how things were; in other words, how things were with my contract being renewed. "Oh, Sue," he said: "I don't see any problems, don't worry." As a non-tenured teacher, you always worry until the first day of your fourth year; then you can breathe. So I went home that day and slept well until five thirty the next morning. That's when our union vice president called me to say I was not rehired. He did not want me going into school blind-sided. I remember hanging up the phone and having to tell Kate. We both sat on the bed in disbelief. Then the tears came and the questions: now what? I got myself together and chose to go in with my head held high. News travels fast according to the sympathetic looks I got immediately on arrival! Those that did not know seemed stunned. The union president and vice president asked me to meet with them and the principal for clarification and options. Looking back, I was in a daze. I'll never forget meeting with Dr. Douche Bag (that's what the kids called him and frankly they weren't far off the mark). He explained how he did not know this would be their decision and how things change at the last minute, blah, blah, blah. All crap. Being in the schools almost twenty years by then, I KNEW these things were planned out ahead of time. I cut the meeting short and went to my office. The kids began hearing and some came to me crying and angry. One girl started a petition. It was done. I had to show up for another month with a smile until the last day of school and I did. I used up a lot of sick time, don't get me wrong. When that last school bell rang, I walked out to my car and was the first to drive out. About a mile down the road, I pulled over and lost it. I shook and cried and screamed; the same behavior as if I saw Marcus. I felt vulnerable and alone. It was not a good day.

The only thing to do was start sending out my resume and wait. The internet made that easier than when I first started teaching. I must have sent out twenty-five to thirty resumes over the next six months; nothing. I sent out more. Nothing. I finally got an interview only because a friend knew a superintendent. I walked into a room with at least a dozen people sitting around a huge conference table. I immediately noticed the stack (and I mean stack) of resumes in front of the building principal. Each person was nice and polite, but my body language skills kicked in quickly. They DID NOT want to be there. This was an obligatory interview; they knew it and I knew it. After about ten minutes (the kiss of death in an interview) they thanked me and I was escorted out by the principal. Before I left, I looked at him and wished him luck with the interviewing. I remember saying, "You have a long day ahead of you. I know I am not your person, and that's okay. Thank you for seeing me." He smiled very kindly and shook my hand. His face said it all. The raised rolling eyes. He did what he had to do with me.

Since the age of twelve, I was never not working. This was a first for me. Months turned into a year. I was becoming depressed and feeling worthless. Kate was supportive, but was growing more concerned, and who could blame her. Unemployment covered my share of the bills, but that was it. I needed good stuff to happen, and it did. The Universe orchestrated several "not by chance encounters" for me during that time. While at a party, a friend told me about a book she was reading called Excuse Me, Your Life is Waiting by Lynn Grabhorn. It was about manifesting things in your life with your thoughts. Another friend told me about The Secret by Rhonda Byrne. Fascinating stuff. Within a week, another friend had a heart-to-heart with me about deserving and the power of our thoughts. I began buying several books and listened to lots of YouTube recordings on positive self-talk and affirmations. "Why not?" I remember thinking. I was a pretty positive person anyway, so this stuff certainly couldn't hurt. And Mom was a big-time believer in positive thinking.

I slowly began absorbing and understanding this Law of Attraction thing and began shifting my thoughts greatly. This time off from working was the perfect opportunity to immerse myself in good stuff. Anytime something "bad" would happen, I would reframe it in my mind and visualize future outcomes. I was hooked.

Mom and I got to spend a lot more time together, and were growing closer. I was now picking her up for doctor's appointments and taking her out shopping and for lunches. It was a good time. My gutsy energetic mother, though, was getting older. I began seeing her as "old." That's not meant to be harsh or insensitive; my protector for my forty plus years on this earth began needing more protecting herself. For the first time, she needed help walking at times, and would wrap her arm into mine for balance. Being a lifelong fast walker, I needed to slow the pace down considerably. And I did. I cleaned her house more and grocery shopped at least two or three times a week. She of course would flip me a twenty or a fifty (which I gladly took, being on unemployment!) I remember sharing concerns about Mom "declining" to my brother and sister. He listened and agreed somewhat; she did not listen and did not want to hear it. "I'll worry about it when the time comes," I remember my sister saying. "The time has come," I responded. With that, I got a quick and dismissive "Sue, I don't want to talk about it." I did not bring it up again. One day Mom and I were having lunch. I was telling her how frustrated I was with the job search and sent out many resumes. The superintendent she knew from years prior was long retired and had no other connections in education. Funny, I was so angry with her for calling him all those years ago, but how I wished she could call somebody now! During one afternoon lunch, Mom said, "Honey, can't you work as a counselor?" Which meant: couldn't I work on my own or in another group practice? "I don't know Mom," was my response. I explained how demanding and uncertain private practice was. The truth being: I was afraid. Private practice was a huge responsibility, never mind financially volatile. I needed a steady paycheck with benefits and a pension. I wanted to wait. Interestingly, our good friends were saying the same thing as Mom. Start your own private practice full-time. I was not listening.

Finally, after over a year, Kate came home from work with interesting news. Kate was now a Psychological Counselor at a local college. Her colleague worked at the college and also part-time at a group practice. She told Kate that the owner was looking for a therapist. I remember her saying, "Why not apply?" My first though was, "Hell, no." I did not want that responsibility. Processing further, I realized beggars could not be choosers. I applied a couple days later. Dolores (the owner) told me at the initial interview she was taking her time in finding "the right person." That was fine with me. The interview, I thought, was awful. I stumbled and was not as articulate as I usually am. I left there, came home and told Kate, "Scratch that one off the list." About a month went by when Dolores called me back for a second interview. I was shocked. I went back and she went into more detail about her expectations and requirements for the job. Again, I stumbled and did not think it went well. A couple more weeks went by and a friend called to say she recommended me for a High School Guidance Counselor job. I was thrilled! I hadn't heard from Dolores, so that was NOT going to happen, and the schools were my life; it's what I knew. I went on the interview for the Guidance job and kicked it! I remember the building principal saying he was impressed with

me and would recommend me to the superintendent of schools (that's the second interview in most school districts, and when that happens, it's a done deal). A few days later, I met with the superintendent. He told me he wanted me and gave me his card. He said I would hear for sure the next day. I was set! Good steady salary again, health benefits and back in the pension plan. The next day...no phone call. I remember thinking "okay, no big deal...he's busy." Something inside me wasn't so sure. The morning after that I got up early and sat on our front porch with my tea and my thoughts. I was saying my positive affirmations, my favorite being, "All is well." Exactly at that moment, my phone rang. It was the superintendent. My heart was racing with excitement. He began by apologizing for not get- ting back to me the day before. "So listen," I remember him saying, "I am so sorry to tell you this, but the job was offered to another candidate." I stuttered with my response, "Oh... oh okay, well that's okay," I remember saying. He went on to explain what had happened, but I couldn't tell you a word of it. I was in shock. I began to cry, but pulled myself together and thanked him for the call. "Of course, if something else comes up, please consider me," I said. And that was that. I sat outside feeling like I was hit by a bus. I could NOT believe this job, which I thought was a sure thing, was gone. Kate was as shocked as I was. She was angry he had "set me up" to believe it was a done deal. I was too. But, in good old Susan fashion, I cried and yelled for a short time, then got up and went back to the drawing board. I went online scoping out guidance counselor jobs.

Life sure does have a way of working itself out. The day AFTER my dream job fell in the crapper, I got a call from Dolores. She wanted to hire me! I was floored! "You what?" I remember saying to her. She laughed. "Yes, Susan, I want you to come work with us." We set up one more meeting so we could discuss salary and begin the process of getting me on insurance panels. I hung up and immediately called Kate. I'll never forget her response when I told her about Dolores' call. "Wait, she wants YOU?" she said with confusion and disbelief. Not "congratulations" or "I'm so proud of you" (those came later) we both laughed as she quickly realized what she said and how she said it."Honey, I'm sorry, I'm just so surprised!" she said. I was too. We hung up and planned a celebration dinner that night. I was officially back in the working world, but it was a world I had never been in before. Group practice had some definite pros. The hours were more flexible and less rigid than working in the schools. I could pretty much make my own schedule. I could see only clients I was

comfortable with. No more formal evaluations, teachers' meetings, teachers' gossip; and those were all good. Then came the cons. In order to make a decent living, I needed to see at least forty people a week (sometimes forty-five). That may sound doable, but let me tell you, it's a grind. I could not see Mom anymore like I had been. I would squeeze in an evening or weekend visit, but to be honest, by the weekends, I was wiped out. She understood and was so sweet. "It's ok, honey, I'm glad you're working. I know I'll see you," I remember her saying. Another con was sitting all day long. I was NOT used to that. Now you might think sitting all day is a great thing. Nope, nope and NOPE! I remember coming home crying because my legs and back hurt. I told Kate I couldn't do this. She agreed the number of clients I was seeing was grossly unrealistic. But I felt I had no choice. I was off unemployment and needed to support myself and our home. I did what I had to do.

I began meeting lots of people with lots of issues. Yes, as a guidance counselor I heard a lot of bad stuff, but this was different. The content of some sessions was intense; it was exhausting, and some were directly hitting on my own past issues. The first thing you learn in the graduate program is be present for the client and put aside any and all personal thoughts and memories. You are there completely for the client and you are paid for a service. I began fine-tuning my skills and finding my identity as a therapist. In meeting other therapists, I came to a quick and solid conclusion: I am not like ANY of these people! No disrespect (or should I say blatant disrespect) to any and all of my colleagues. My style seemed so very different from theirs. Different theoretic orientations teach you different things; how to act, what to say and how to say it. I am SO a non-conformist! I laugh a lot during session, share personal stories, even curse from time to time. My favorite line is: "Yes, I went to school for this, but I am in the same boat you are...trying to figure it all out." I knew early in my counseling career I wanted to be "real." I settled into life as a full-time psychotherapist. I was now paying it forward (or "gaying" it forward) giving my clients the guidance and assurance that my own therapists gave me. That part was, and still is, very cool.

CHAPTER TWELVE

A TIME TO LAUGH, A TIME TO CRY...

It was October, and it was Mom's eightieth birthday. The year earlier, while having cake for her seventy-ninth birthday, she told my brother, my sister and I that she was throwing herself an eightieth birthday party. "Now listen kids, I'll take care of everything, you just show up," she said. Sounded great to us. Considering everything she had gone through with her own mother and losing my Dad and all of my stuff, she deserved a big fat bash. So for the next year Mom and I talked about a venue, invitations, food and music. She was so excited. She was like a little kid who couldn't wait for the day to arrive. Without exaggeration, almost every morning phone conversation we had that whole year had something to do with her big birthday party! "Now Sue...should I have chicken or pork, or both? Where should we get the paper for the invitations?" And it went on and on. At times I remember rolling my eyes on the other end of the phone saying to myself "not again!" But deep in my core I knew Mom was not long for this world as I had consistently witnessed her changes. Every time I wanted to scream "we talked about that already!" I shut my mouth and did what I could to listen. I hope I did. Mom took the bull by the horns and planned. She called a local event hall and asked her friends for DJ recommendations. We slowly bought decorations, and she began making seating charts. And damn it if she didn't take care of EVERYTHING. We went to the venue at least two or three times to make sure it was just right. And then there was "the speech." Mom wanted to make a speech to thank all of us and her family and friends for being part of her special day. She read it to me over and over, day after day. Again, sometimes it was hard to listen, but you know what? I can't imagine how many times I repeated my spelling words as a child or rambled on and on about nonsense kid stuff. She was worth it. The invites went out, all was in place.

The big day finally arrived. Kate and I got to Mom's house early that Sunday. She was wearing a beautiful gold sequined top, black dress slacks and her best jewelry. She had on her signature red lipstick. She looked absolutely regal. I could tell she was nervous, because she was a woman who did nothing quickly. She always took her time deciding and doing.

That morning, she was buzzing through her house. I took her hands and simply said, "Mom, we are here. "I know honey," she said, as she smiled and patted my cheek. We loaded party stuff into the car and off we went. Mom had asked us to pick up her birthday cake from a local bakery. Sure thing, no problem. "Now it might be a little big," I remember her saying. Kate and I looked at each other as if to say, "How big could it possibly be?" We left Mom at the hall with the wait staff and drove to the bakery. I handed over the receipt and they said they would box it right away. "Do you need us to put this in your car?" I remember the woman saying. "Ah, no," I responded.

Again, how big could it be? Then the woman brought out this monster size box; I thought someone was going to jump out of it! IT WAS HUGE! I stood there for a second, started to laugh, and then simply said, "Well, ok... thank you!" I went out to the car and got Kate. She couldn't understand why I needed her help. Then she saw the box. We both laughed. The box barely fit into the back of my Honda. I had to sit back there holding it so it would not tip over. The stress was palpable.

I KNEW Mom would be upset if something happened to the cake. I barked at Kate to drive extra slow taking every side street we could. With flashers on, Kate maneuvered every pothole and every turn. I admit I gave Kate a lot of crap that day, but I just wanted to get the cake there safely. I am proud to report we did! We walked in carrying this huge box. Mom's eyes popped open. "Wow, that's big," she said. We set it down and opened the box. It had lovely pink and yellow flowers with a big inscription "Happy Birthday Vicky." Mom was pleased. My brother and sister and their families arrived shortly after, and we did everything "The General" (Mom) asked us to do. Thank God the bar was open!

When the guests began to arrive, Mom was in her glory. She showed everyone to the table with the seating cards and directed her guests to the coat room and to the bar. The DJ had arrived while we were picking up the cake and was playing soft oldies music. I remember it feeling strange because so many family members had passed on. Dad was one of ten children and Mom was one of six. My Aunt Reggie and Aunt Josie had both passed away a few years prior. I know she was missing them most of all that day. Mom's friends arrived with flowers and gifts and smiles. She insisted the food be ready, so the buffet line

AS I WAS HOLDING HER HAND, SHE SQUEEZED MINE AND SMILED. AND THEN SHE WAS GONE

got started right away. The music pumped up, the bar was swarming with my cousins and Mom's friends. The polka dancing was in full swing. Mom and I danced several songs. I was more out-of-breath then she was! Then came 'the speech'. Now remember I had heard this speech a whole lot of times before. But there Mom stood; microphone in hand, sparkling in the DJ's lighting. She looked like a queen. She thanked all of us for being there and for the love she had felt for so long. I watched her talk. Verbally, she was articulate and humble. Physically, I saw this old lady standing up there. I started to cry not at what she was saying, but with this assurance that things were indeed changing. Maybe I was worrying for nothing. Mom's own mother lived to be ninety-three. I shook my head and stayed in the moment. When Mom was finished, everyone stood up and toasted her. Some people gave her well wishes in Polish. And she deserved it! The monster cake was lit and we sang Happy Birthday. Mom cut everyone's slice. As the guests began to leave, we dutifully thanked everyone for coming. I remember Mom saying, "Wow, that went by fast." And she was right. All the planning and talking over the last year was over before we knew it. We brought Mom home, along with the extra food, birthday cake and presents. When we left, the kitchen table and counter were completely covered. The next day I called Mom at our usual morning time. She was sleepy. She must have thanked me four or five times for my efforts in making the party memorable. She said "I know you did so much, Sue, I couldn't have done it without you."

Christmas that year came and went. Mom was growing more tired, more often. Her appetite was changing, too. She would go for days not eating much more than Special K cereal. She ordered presents online for home delivery and I picked up whatever I could. I did the holiday dinner shopping, too. Mom just wasn't able to. I again tried talking with my brother and sister. My brother was becoming more concerned, but did not know what to do. My sister still did not want to hear it. Anyway, Mom had made it clear for years; she would NOT be put in a nursing home and most recently said she did not need a live-in or even a part-time caregiver. As usual, we abided by her wishes. She wanted to live in her own house and die there when her time came. I remember telling her if she ever needed, I would quit my job and take care of her. Instead of a gracious, "Oh honey, thank you," she angrily responded with the accusation that I was taking her money, and that she was offended I would even suggest such a thing! I was floored. She did not want to talk about it anymore. And that was that. I told my brother who then tried to reiterate my conversation

with Mom. She cut him off, too. I had pushed a major hot button. I apologized and that was that.

I started taking Mom to more doctors' appointments; something she had done completely on her own. Even the dentist. She wanted me there with her anytime it was possible, and would schedule her appointments around my work schedule. Looking back, it may have been a growing fear of driving. Maybe it was her balance. Anytime I asked how she was feeling, the answer was the same: "I'm fine...fine, fine, fine." We had gotten her one of those elder alert buttons to push in case she fell, and up until then, it was on her dresser gathering dust. I looked at her one day with tears in my eyes and said, "If anything ever happened to you where you fell and were alone, I would never get over it." For the first time, she heard me and from that day on she wore the pendant religiously. And if it wasn't around her neck, it was next to her night stand. Easter that year was going to be the typical Polish Easter with Kielbasa and stuffed cabbage and potatoes (can't ever leave out the potatoes). Her appetite seemed to be improving and she seemed happy for the holiday to arrive and for us to be together. Two days before Easter, Mom called to tell me she fell. I rushed to her house and found her on the TV room floor propped up against the couch. She was alert and seemed fine otherwise. I helped her up onto the couch and tried to deduce what happened. "I don't know honey, my legs just gave way, like dominoes," she said. She called her primary doctor who thought it was dehydration or a medication issue. He could not see her for several days, so we decided to go to a walk-in clinic for a glucose test. She absolutely would NOT let me call an ambulance. I was by myself and was starting to freak out. She had regained her strength and we walked to the car and arrived at the clinic. After waiting over an hour, we were told they could not test her sugar because "they ran out of strips." Mom and I looked at each other in disbelief. "Are you serious?" I said. The young nurse who delivered the news was apologetic and embarrassed. Then she left the room. Since the emergency room was still out of the question, I drove Mom home and decided to spend the night. I called my brother and filled him in on the day's events. "Well, how is she?" I remember him asking. "Okay, I guess, but I really don't know." Her speech became slightly garbled. My brother came over that night after work. He and Mom talked about her health (she always seemed to listen to him more than my sister and me). She was looking and sounding much better, so we all thought it was just a freak thing. My brother went home and I called Kate to tell her I wouldn't be home. I remember Kate suggesting we go

to the ER, but this was my mother we were talking about; old or not, she was the boss. When she said no, it was NO. I helped her to the bathroom several times before I put her to bed. I slept on the TV room sofa in earshot of Mom's room. If I got two hours of sleep that night, it was a lot. "Sue, Sue...." Mom called out more than once. And each time, I leapt off the couch and rushed to her bed. She seemed okay, just needing help going to the bathroom. It is a very sobering moment to help your parent off with their clothes and tend to their proper hygiene after using the toilet. I didn't mind any of it, but I admit to crying after helping her back to bed. The morning came and Mom got up on her own. I had gone to the bagel store to get her French toast and a sandwich for lunch. I had to go to work. She seemed much better than the night before. She promised to wear her alert button and call me later. I reluctantly left.

That day was uneventful. I must have called Mom five or six times, and each time, she said the same thing: "I am fine." She said she slept a lot and spoke with friends on the phone. I decided to spend the night again and returned to Mom's house after work. She really seemed okay, sitting on the loveseat eating cookies. Her appetite had been off again. As the night before, I helped her around the house, into the bathroom, washing in the bathtub. Mom was fiercely independent and looking back this must have been humiliating for her. That night, she told me she didn't want to have Easter dinner. "Honey, I'm just not up for it this year," she said. I remember getting this sick feeling in my stomach. That was NOT Mom. I called my brother and sister to tell them. Despite Mom's request, we decided to meet at Mom's house anyway Easter Sunday and do our best. Mom put on a brave face, but barely ate the Polish food she had enjoyed all her life. When I sheepishly brought up Mom using a walker, she jumped at the idea. "I think that's a good idea, honey. Are the stores open today?" I found a drug store open on Easter Sunday and came back with a sapphire blue walker. We put it together and showed Mom how to use it. She maneuvered it like a champ!

Much to my surprise, things were quite calm after that. For the next two months Mom regained her strength, began shopping and driving and was even going to the gym where she would swim with her "lady friend." It really was as if nothing happened! I caught up on my sleep, reconnected with Kate and our cats and went back to normal life. Mom even took me out for my birthday that June. We sat in the diner and talked about Kate and I deciding to get married. She was happy and offered to help. Then came July. After working about ten hours on a Tuesday and seeing eleven

clients back to back, the phone rang around 10:30. It was Mom.

"Honey, could you come over, I fell." I told her I would be there and hung up the phone. I started to get out of bed and realized I could not do this by myself. I called my brother and he agreed to go to Mom's house. About a half hour later, I called Mom. "Hi, honey, your brother is here," I remember her saying. I spoke with her briefly, then him. He said that Mom started to get up off the couch and her legs crumbled under her. He would spend the night and I would go the next morning. I hung up the phone, and Kate held me. I was upset.

The next morning, I called out of work and got to Mom in time for my brother to leave. Mom had a peaceful night and was eating Special K. When I told my brother I was spending the day and night there, I remember him saying, "You really don't have to...she's okay." Something else was telling me otherwise and I politely told him I was staying. Mom and I spent that day talking, laughing, and watching her favorite shows. I cleaned and picked up lunch from the bagel shop. Evening came. She used her walker like a pro with me walking behind her like a nervous parent hovering over a child. This was becoming our routine, me spending the night helping Mom when she needed the bathroom. The next day she woke up and used the walker into the kitchen. As I was walking behind her, her legs gave way. Catching your parents in your arms is a surreal experience. She was all weight, and letting go was not an option. I helped her to the chair and sat with her for a couple minutes. Like the other times, she soon regained strength. She maneuvered around the house and decided to lie down. I told her I would go get groceries and be back within the hour. "Don't worry, honey, I'm fine," I remember her saying. I left and got to the supermarket. I was only there about ten minutes, when my cell phone rang. It was Mom. I was certain she wanted to add something to the shopping list as she was not shy to call me when she needed something. "Honey, I fell again." I quickly paid for the groceries and tore back to her house. She was on the floor in the bedroom. This time, I could not get her up. Luckily, the neighbor was home and we were able to help Mom onto the bed. When the neighbor left, Mom wanted to make her way to the TV room. Again I walked behind her as she used the walker. And again her legs gave way. Catch number two for Susan. I sat her down, looked her in the eyes and said, "Mom, we have to go." She knew what I meant. I called 911 and within five minutes the ambulance arrived. I remember gathering whatever Mom told me to: toothbrush, nightgown, and slippers. I held her purse and made sure she had her cell phone and charger. The EMS guys could not have been nicer, calling her beautiful and a youngster. She liked that. Mom's only request was that they not put on the siren. We went through too much of that with Dad. They honored her request. I called my brother from the ambulance and off we went.

It was quickly deduced by the emergency room physician that Mom had atrial fibrillation and needed additional tests. One of those tests showed an eighty percent heart blockage and Mom needed bypass surgery. She was moved to a different hospital within two days. I met Mom the morning she was transported and spent the day at her bedside. We had breakfast and lunch together and met several nurses and doctors. The heart surgeon popped in to introduce himself and quickly go through the surgery details. Mom was alert and asked questions. "I have a couple of surgeries tomorrow, so I may not get to you right away. But that's a good thing, you are not a priority," I remember the surgeon saying. Mom seemed relieved (and so was I). After dinner, I told Mom I needed to leave and kissed her goodnight. She seemed fine and was resting comfortably. Early the next morning, my brother called to say Mom had a "bad night" and was being prepped for surgery right away. It's funny how fast things can happen. My brother, sister and I got to the hospital in time to see Mom in the holding room. She was sedated and pretty out of it. I lost it. I cried and kissed her. "Oh, honey," Mom mumbled, "I am just fine." We were asked to leave and found our way to the common waiting area. The volunteers could not have been nicer, explaining where the cafeteria was and showing us "the board." It was like being in an airport; Mom had a number, and we got to "track" when she entered surgery and when she was done. It was agony waiting (as any of you know) but after only a few hours, the surgeon came out and said everything went beautifully. Mom was responding well and would be released to a rehabilitation center in a few days. All was good. We were allowed to see her for a short time in the recovery room. She was hooked up to lots of buzzing beeping machines and was still out of it from the anesthesia. I remember falling into my brother's arms. We each took turns holding Mom's hand telling her everything was okay. No response. The nurse said that was normal. We were told to go home since Mom would be sleeping most of that day and night. I went home and fell into Kate's arms. The next day, we returned to the hospital. Mom was still groggy, but her eyes were open and she was able to squeeze our hands. Even though she didn't look good, we were assured she was headed in the right direction. She was transferred to the

CCU unit from post-op ICU and spent the next eight days there. The anesthesia really knocked her out. She was combative at times, scattered in thoughts and words other times. She could not brush her teeth, brush her hair, or wipe her face. The nurses were amazing, but they simply could not do everything; and I did not expect them to. After some predicted complications, Mom was transferred to a rehabilitation facility.

"All she needs is to build up her strength and she will be fine," one doctor said. My brother was with Mom when she got to the rehab center, and I arrived shortly after. Mom wanted clothes and other personals from her house. I remember getting to her house that day and opening her back door. The house was quiet and cold and empty. I froze and lost it. I sobbed and sobbed sitting right where she used to sit. I was tired and scared. I wiped the tears, went into her bedroom and bathroom, and got everything she wanted. I returned to the rehab and she was sleeping. I just sat with her. It was all I could do. Each day Mom was up and down. Some days she would go to physical therapy, most days not. She was barely eating. I brought her those fruity protein shakes. I remember one day she wanted an ice cream, so I dashed out and returned with a vanilla fudge sundae. When she was able, she talked on her cell phone to friends, but mostly she slept. Day after day, I would watch the Classic Movie Channel as well as watch Mom sleep. I was working full-time too. When I was at work, I would call her and often leave a voicemail message. One Saturday around 5:30 am, Mom called. Her voice was garbled and almost inaudible; "Honey, can you come here, I want to quit this place," she said. I was startled and confused. I hung up and started getting dressed. Kate was awakened by the phone and said, "Susan, you aren't really going are you?" "Of course I am," I said. "I'll call you later." I remember taking the forty-minute drive down the streets I had come to know well. The sun was rising just as I got to the rehab. It was a beautiful morning. A doctor let me in and I walked down to Mom's room. "Hi honey," she said. Didn't you just leave?" "No, Mom, it's morning." "Well you'd better leave before it gets dark." I think she was confused with morning and evening. I sat with her and listened to her talk about wanting to leave the facility and not feeling sure what to do. After a few minutes, she looked at me and said, "You know what? I want to stay here. It's okay. "And that was that. She smiled and closed her eyes to sleep. She awoke briefly and told me to go home and that she was okay. She insisted. I called my brother on the way home and he agreed to visit her that afternoon. I told him I would return the next day by early afternoon. "Sue, you really don't have to...this is a marathon, not a sprint,"

I remember him saying. "Stay home for a few days, we got this." As tempting as that was and despite how everyone around me was saying to slow down, I knew I wanted to see Mom the next day. Sunday morning. I got up and got ready. I stopped at a local deli to pick up a breakfast sandwich and iced tea. As I was leaving the deli, a song was playing on the radio about letting go and how things were going to work out. I stopped dead in my tracks there in the doorway. Something came over me; a calm peaceful feeling. "Let it go and let it flow...everything's going to work out right ya know." I smiled and left there feeling more optimistic and assured than I had in many months. Mom was going to be okay. When I got to her room she was lying in the bed breathing heavily and sweating. My brother was there along with a nurse. The nurse assured us Mom was fine and that this kind of thing happened sometimes when patients get up out of bed. I called out "morning matka" (good morning mother in Polish) and leaned in to kiss Mom on the forehead. In a very soft voice she said "I am so glad you are here." I smiled and assured her I was there for the whole day and to rest. My brother needed to take his sons to their sports games. "It's all good, don't worry, I got this," I said to him. He leaned in and kissed Mom goodbye saying, "You got to get better, okay?" "Okay," she said. After my brother left, I gave Mom some ice water and wiped her face down with a cool cloth. She said her side was hurting, so I got an ice pack from the nurse's station and placed it on her rib cage. Her breathing leveled out and she was quieter and more still than when I first arrived. Then all of a sudden her eyes got big and wide. She was pointing up to the television. I kept asking her what she saw. She mumbled. I knew she saw someone there. After that, she said she was going to go. My heart dropped. I wasn't sure what to do. I held her hand and rubbed her arm. Through my tears, I asked her if she was going to dance at my wedding in a few months. "No," she said. Then she made me laugh by saying, "I don't care...well, I do care." I wanted to tell her it was okay to go but I was terrified. Instead while holding her hand; I said it to her in my mind. I told her telepathically it was okay to go and see Daddy. Right at that moment she said one more time: "I'm gonna go now." Her breathing slowed considerably. As I was holding her hand, she squeezed mine and smiled. And then she was gone. I was panicked and stunned and shaking. I stood up and looked at her staring straight ahead. I lifted her arm only to have it slam down on the bed. I noticed her left arm was blue. I remember standing there shaking and sobbing. A nurse came a few moments later, and barely able to speak I said, "I think she's dead." The nurse screamed

down the hall and a barrage of staff came flying in. They asked me to step out. I heard them say DNR or no DNR. I remembered what that meant from Dad's many hospital stays. I heard them asking for a crash cart. That's when I went back into the room and screamed: "NO, don't... please let her be." Mom was lying flat this time looking more lifeless than a few minutes prior. I was escorted out of the room and into the hallway. I was alone. One woman visiting her mother across the hall came out and comforted me. She was so nice. A few minutes later, the head nurse came out and told me Mom had indeed passed away. With her arms around me, we walked down to her office.

Just like Mom had to call the family to inform them of Dad's passing some twenty-six years earlier, it was my job to do it for her. The first person I called was Kate. When she picked up the phone I simply said, "Honey, shine your shoes." That is a phrase our friends use when someone has died and a wake and funeral are in the works. "Wait, what?" I remember her saying. I could barely get out more words. I asked her to call our friends as I needed to call my brother and sister. She was concerned about me being alone and having to drive home. "I'm okay, don't worry, "I remember saying to her. Even though I wasn't. Then I called my brother. When I told him she was "gone" (I purposely did not use the word died) he was speechless. He breathed heavily into the phone and immediately asked if I was ok. I told him I would arrange for Mom to be brought to the funeral home my Dad was laid out in. I then called my sister. "No, NO," my sister kept saying. All I could muster back was "Yes. We'll call you later." The nurse had me sign some papers and informed a staff member to collect Mom's belongings. It felt like hours. They came out of her room with a trash bag and a shopping bag of clothes, pictures and personals. Just two days before, I had washed and ironed all of Mom's shirts and slacks so they would look nice and placed the neatly folded piles in her closet. Mom always liked it when things were ironed. I walked to my car with bags in hand. I was so upset about leaving her there alone. It was a beautiful sunny afternoon. I drove and cried and yelled and wailed. The angels guided my driving that day, for sure, because I do not remember one lick of the ride. When I got home, Kate was waiting at the front door. When she saw me, she took the bags from my hands and helped me into the house. We sat in the living room, our cats curiously smelling me. What was there to say, really? She kept saying she couldn't believe it, and I kept saying I knew it...I just knew it. We had to plan. My brother came over later that afternoon and we sat on our back deck drinking single malt scotch. Our previous conversations of Mom's possible need for long-term care were now replaced with discussions of her wake and funeral.

The next morning we planned to meet my sister at the funeral home. Before that, I met my brother at Mom's house to collect needed papers and banking information. It was the shittiest experience of my life to walk back into that house without her there. It was one thing going there while she was in the hospital, but this time she was never coming back. We didn't stay long. Looking back, I think we both wanted to get in and out. We met my sister and listened to the funeral director talk about options, expenses, and the rest of the "happy horse shit" as my father used to say. Luckily, the three of us agreed on mostly everything. When he asked about an obituary I had informed my brother and sister I had written one many months before. I know it sounds macabre, but I KNEW I needed to do it before she was actually gone. When I started to see Mom changing, I began writing. I needed to be clearheaded and not forget anything important. We arranged for the wake and funeral to be in three days. We went back to Mom's house and just sat there. It was weird. I went back to the house several times by myself before the wake and funeral. I needed to lie on Mom's bed and cry. I needed to remember her sitting on the couch in the TV room. I even sat on the floor where she had fallen as if to connect with her in some way. What I really needed was her alive again. Looking back, I am so glad I went back there as often as I did; not for closure exactly, but for clarity. Mourning is a personal process.

Her wake was held in the same room as Dad's was twenty-six years earlier. The room was beautiful with flowers and cards. As we walked up to the casket, I immediately smiled. Kate was surprised I was smiling and not crying. Mom looked beautiful! Her hair and makeup were exactly as when she was alive. Her nails were a pretty soft pink. Right now as I write this, I am laughing. Mom HATED when people said "how good" someone looked at their wake. "They're dead!" I remember she would say. "How good can they look?" Let me tell you, Mom looked GOOD. I cannot thank the funeral home enough for that. The vision of her lifeless body the day she died is one I will never forget. My brother and sister and their spouses and children mingled and meandered around the room until people began to arrive. Everyone was shocked and some asked a lot of questions. All I could say was it was her time to go and she died peacefully. I got to talk through that last day with Mom which turned out to be quite therapeutic. The funeral came and went and Mom was buried with

Dad. The repass was at a Polish restaurant in the town where Mom grew up. Seemed fitting.

The days, weeks and months to follow were about probating Mom's will, finances, all the stuff no one prepares you for when you lose your last parent. All in all, my brother and I worked well together and agreed on almost everything. I went to Mom's house frequently for practical and personal reasons. When the day came to put it up for sale, I did not think I could bear it. Seeing that sign on the front lawn nearly ripped my heart out. Interesting, though, something happened that was a blessing in the midst of my anguish. Kate had told me about a psychic/medium she had known years earlier. She liked her and said she was spot on. I had seen several psychics before and enjoyed the experience. So what the hell, right? It turns out visiting Lorraine was exactly what I needed. She told me Mom was in God's light and her soul was at peace. She told me Mom was not afraid while she was dying. Without my prompting, she told me that Mom saw my father the day she died and was happy to go with him. She told me Mom passed over while I was holding her hand. I sobbed and cheered. All good news! Then she abruptly stopped talking and said, "What...?" She was looking behind me. I admit I was freaked! She explained Mom was standing behind me and wanted me to know (and I am quoting Lorraine now): "I looked pretty good for a dead woman!" I burst out laughing. Lorraine was confused and when she asked why I was laughing, I told her about Mom's disdain for saying that people looked good at wakes. Lorraine laughed, too. "Oh, now it makes sense!" Your Mom said she knows she rode you with that while she was alive." When I told Lorraine about Mom's anger over my suggestion that I take care of her, she immediately spoke out and said, "Your mother was a very proud woman, very independent." True. "She never wanted to burden you kids with taking care of her. Your Mom is telling me she knew you would have done it, but she didn't want you to give up your life that way." I was pleased and relieved to hear that. Believe in psychics or not, but all those words soothed my swirling mind. Lorraine then asked about Mom's house and assured me Mom wanted it to be sold. "Your Mom is saying it's just a house, let it go. She doesn't want you to be burdened with it." Music to my ears. Even though I was inching my way to accepting the impending house sale more and more, hearing her words was my final push. I left that session feeling lighter, clearer and very, very grateful. Mom's house sold a few months later to a young family with two small girls. At the closing, the couple thanked me for giving them

Mom's house (my brother and sister could not attend) and how happy their girls were to live in "the little yellow house with the pink bedroom." There was life once more.

Kate and I were married three months later and most recently I opened my very own counseling office. Mom always said I was "the kind of person" to be self-employed. Still not sure what that means, but I choose to take it as a compliment. To be honest, it really is nice to do it "my way" to quote an old Blue Eyes song. Life has been very different with Mom not in it and I still struggle with talking about her. But just as my father's passing brought clarity and light with Marcus, Mom's passing has given me the courage to write. Wherever she is right now, I know she is proudly showing off this book. That's who she is.

Last picture of me and Mom. She died one month later.

CHAPTER THIRTEEN
OH HAPPY DAY...

Writing this book has been everything from cathartic to nerve-wracking to humorous to haunting. I admit there were times I did not want to keep going. "What's the point in dredging all this up again?" was a continuing theme running through my head. Something inside me, though, kept bumping the "whys" out of the way and replacing them with "keep writing." It wasn't until I was almost finished when a strong unwavering realization came over me: we are all more similar than different. The content of my story may be different than yours, but the feelings and emotions and struggles are eerily alike. And the only thing that has kept me from ending my time here on this earth was knowing that I am the power that controls that life; not Marcus, not the church, not my father or mother, but me. I get to decide how I feel, what I believe, how I act. Learning about the Law of Attraction and the powers of choice and gratitude have literally saved my life and they can save yours, too.

The Law of Attraction is a law of the Universe; just like the Law of Gravity. With gravity, if we drop something, it will immediately or eventually fall. It is law. Doesn't matter if you are good or bad or right or wrong. The Law of Attraction is similar in that we attract what we give out. Like a magnet that attracts a like current or a radio station tuned into a certain frequency. Our thoughts are like that magnet and will attract good or bad things depending on their content. If you remember, I really got into this law when I was unemployed. That crappy period in my life turned out to be a blessing in that I had time to learn and process and put into practice this interesting law of the Universe. It is about believing in our core that we DESERVE peace and abundance and love and ease. One great teacher uses the word "ease" a lot, which I recommend you do as well. A client recently said: "Ok Susan, so you're saying all I have to do is think good thoughts and believe I deserve and my life will turn around?" "Yes," I replied simply. With practice and commitment our lives WILL turn around. It is law.

The biggest challenge for most of us is our willingness to reprogram our brains. It's not that we can't reprogram; many of us are scared to death! Not to be disrespectful to any organized religion, but many believe that by practicing the Law of Attraction, the wrath of God or a horrific wave of punishment will come upon us. I have heard this over and over again. I felt it too. Being raised Catholic, I was taught this was THE religion. Period. And if I did not believe what I was taught, I was bad or damned. So out of fear (and only fear) I remained loyal to my church. I also remained loyal to my parents who introduced me to my church. I felt I was slapping them in the face if I leaned towards any other teachings. It has nothing to do with believing in God; I ABSOLUTELY believe in God (which I call Spirit). It is about believing in OURSELVES and the power WE have with our thoughts and beliefs. Thoughts are energy and energy is incredibly strong, both good and bad.

In Chapter One I talked about blame. I have come to believe that blame and resentment and frustration are all chosen emotions that we can control. We can choose these or not. We can choose how long to "stay there." I don't begrudge anyone these feelings in dealing with life events; on the contrary, I encourage my clients to get mad and blame and be resentful and frustrated. I believe it is necessary to purge in order to heal. I have many photographs with holes in them as proof of my own expressions of anger. Think of it this way: If we feel nauseous, by throwing up we purge the toxins and once we do, we feel better. Looking back I spent a lot of time blaming my parents and the church and my coworkers and my lovers for everything wrong in my life. I displaced my personal responsibility on them. It wasn't wrong of me to feel this way; I just stayed Oh Happy Day...! there too long. I learned in my own therapy that letting go is THE MOST powerful tool in the healing process. It's a challenging path; a path that wants to take you back to the bad stuff and leave you there. One teacher said it so perfectly: it's like going to the buffet table and taking foods you hate. You moan and groan and complain that the food is terrible. And what do you do? You go back to the SAME buffet table and take the SAME food over and over! Sounds crazy to intentionally choose the bad; but when you think for a minute, that's what we all do! We keep reliving and rehashing and readdressing our past traumas and hurts over and over again. As I said before, it is NECESSARY to relive and revisit somewhat. But then there NEEDS to be a time to put it down. I ask my clients to imagine themselves carrying around a twenty pound rock. They are carrying it all day, every day. And when I ask them "what could you do to feel better?" they matter of factly say to me, "Put it down." RIGHT! Put it down. We can choose to put down our old stuff and live comfortably and more easily.

Looking back and reflecting now, the biggest person I blamed for what happened with Marcus was me. One hundred percent. The church said it, my mother initially said it. It did not mean they were right, it meant that I chose to accept that as truth. The Church made it clear to my attorney they believed I was an active participant in my abuse. Being female (don't forget I was twelve) in some way I enabled this man to molest me. Remember when my attorney told me they thought I was a gold digger? So in their eyes, I was a sexual manipulator as well as a money whore. At first I was enraged that my attorney told me what they thought of me. I remember thinking, "What good did it do to tell me that?" Actually, it did A LOT of good. I went from being angry and resentful at all those involved, to feeling grateful; very grateful. Through the Law of Attraction, I realized that I got to choose how I view myself. I decided what was true. I had the biggest say in what Susan REALLY was; and the heck with anyone else who thought otherwise. Now don't get me wrong, this took time and work. I had to reprogram years of past messages and skewed rhetoric. I had to STOP putting so much energy into them and their thoughts and beliefs about me, and start using my energy for my good. It is always a choice. See, that's the thing. We can't change what people think or believe about us. NOTHING we say or do will change someone unless they themselves make it happen. Do we try to change people? ALL THE TIME! We explain, we argue, we debate, all in the hopes we can convince them of something else. Newsflash: it's a waste of our energy!

I also mentioned grooming and programming throughout the book; both real and calculated methods used by perpetrators. I know now I was conditioned. It was out of my hands. I was young and vulnerable and naïve (and Marcus preyed on that). He could have chosen to love me in a healthy nurturing way. Instead, he groomed me into his idea of who I should be and conditioned me to respond the way he wanted. Any abuse survivors reading this needs to believe what I am saying here. Blaming yourself for sexual abuse is as ludicrous as blaming a toddler for falling down as he learns to walk. No one would call that child "stupid" or hold them responsible. Life is learning, and when we learn certain things early by authority figures, those patterns continue. I spent way too much time and energy with one simple word: "why?" Why did Marcus do what he did? Why did the Church turn their heads? Why did those other

WHAT WE CHOOSE TO DO IT UP TO US

men choose to molest me, too? Why did my father get sick? Why did Mom blame me when I told her? Why ME? All the time and emotional energy I spent on the "whys" could have been used for my greater good. What happened happened. I could not wish it away or curse it away or even drink it away. It was and still is part of my history. So instead of marinating in it, I started to ask myself, "Now what?" I have today, and what I do with today is up to ME, not anyone else. The past really is over and done with and my present and future can be anything I choose (I really believe that). Again, my friends, this does not mean we should not get angry. Get angry, cry and scream...Then, just like the twenty pound rock...put it down.

I mentioned earlier about my exceptional talent in reading body Oh Happy Day...! language. I would not have this now if not for my past. And I am grateful for it. My clients are blown away when I question a response they give or ask them to answer a question again. Some try so hard to skirt the issue by meandering around it, hoping I buy the load of dung they are shoveling. Nope, not me. As a gentle persuader, I delicately steer them back. Some are not happy, but most are eventually grateful. Let's face it, no one WANTS to go back to a time, or many many times that were horrific and traumatic. No one wants to relive. My approach, however, is just that. In order to heal NOW, we must address THEN. Not live there, setting up camp, but go back for a time and relive it OUR way. With respect to my colleagues who do not believe in working through the past, I think that's a load of hooey. Some therapists are strictly "here and now" people. The same maladaptive behaviors keep repeating over and over until we get to the root of why they are there in the first place. Even more importantly, why we CHOOSE to keep them there. We all know lying, cheating, stealing, and hurting are bad things. Yet we ALL choose to do them over and over. My strong belief is we do what we think we deserve. Think about it. If we grew up in a household where we were told we sucked or we were stupid or we would never amount to anything, and then end up harming others physically or emotionally, that is not by accident! Early programming gave us an idea of our personal worth. A belief system not created by you, but by well-meaning people who repeated their own past programming. We have the choice to continue believing such nonsense, or we can create OUR OWN belief system about ourselves. I know...easier said than done; but by no means impossible.

I have a wonderful client who came to me with a laundry list of past

trauma. She was depressed and felt hopeless. For the first several sessions, I listened and validated. I told her how awful her past must have been. She was grateful for the validation. When I started to discuss how she deserved a happy life and regain control, she became angry and hostile. I remember her saying in one session, "You don't understand how much I have been through. You don't care!" I again validated her years of trauma and clarified, "You have every right to be angry and resentful, and I want you to feel it." Her demeanor changed quickly and she asked to end the session and reschedule. We set up another appointment and she left. A few days later, I got an email from her along with notice she was canceling all future visits. The email blasted me for being unfeeling and matter of fact. She felt mistreated (like with so many others in her life). I remember reading the email admittedly feeling angry and frustrated. I worked hard with her only to be blasted as not caring. But that was not it at all. I quickly realized she was reacting to my kindness and compassion (something she had not had) and also reacting to the word "deserve. "As soon as I said that word, the switch flipped. Her anger was not really at me, but at a life that was slipping through her fingers. And until she believed for herself that she deserved joy and love and peace, it was not going to come and things were not going to change. Interestingly, I spoke with her former therapist (having permission of course) and was told this client had marinated in the past for years. She chose to "stay there."

Another current client has more resolve than anger. Jane and I have worked together almost three years. She is by far one of the strongest women I know (although she thinks I am crazy for believing that). Her family history reads like a chilling horror novel. Multiple abuses, daily ridicule, prostituting her out, the list goes on and on. And yet, she continues her therapy. She likes to "skirt the issues" like so many others, and I gently bring her back each time. One day with a sad lost look on her face she said, "Am I broke beyond repair...am I THAT damaged?" Never in twenty-five years as a therapist have I had such a reaction. I fought back tears. I cleared my throat over and over. After a brief silence, I simply said, "Of course not...you are Jane...and Jane deserves to be happy." She looked at me with the eyes of a child hearing a foreign language. She was distant in that session; looking completely defeated. As much as I encourage her and validate her, she chooses to believe she is not worthy and deserving of good. She gets that the past is over and that her parents made some horrific choices with her and for her, but she allows that past to continue Oh Happy Day...! to identify her now. There is no question that some of us have more layers than others; insidious harmful layers that have permeated our psyches. But here again, as with myself and so many clients I have worked with, we all really CAN choose our life path. As with the previous client, Jane still does not accept that she deserves a happy life.

Deserve. Hmmm......let's discuss. In all my years of asking clients if they "truly deserve" to be happy, only a handful have responded with a resounding "Yes!" That means most of us are saying, "No." Some have responded "Yes" right away but their body language screams, "NO." Why is it that so many of us do not embrace our deservedness? Past conditioning? Past trauma? Both probably true. All the more reason to work through those old layers and put them down. Feeling like we deserve is a choice, plain and simple. Once we do, deserving is not just a concept, it is a certainty. We need to CHOOSE to get there and CHOOSE to stay there. CHOOSE to look into the mirror and say affirming statements (mirror work is fabulous and quite empowering). CHOOSE to believe in ourselves when others did not. It takes practice, and it does not happen overnight. It can be frustrating when we want to get there SO badly and feel like we are strolling instead of sprinting. Believe me, I GET IT! At the same time, this amazing life we have gives us all we need to accomplish our dreams.

The crux of my therapy with clients is getting them to see the power THEY have. After working through layers of past trauma, I often say, "Now what?" during sessions. I can't tell you how many thousands of stunned sets of eyes have looked back at me after saying that! It's as if there is no "now what" because the power of the damage remains. I have my clients look at old pictures and mementos from those who have hurt them. The fear, the utter fear that envelopes most is astounding. I too, had that fear when I began picture work with Marcus. But boy does it work! The eventual freedom and power we achieve by expressing OUR feelings is magnificent. That piece of paper or jewelry or whatever holds SUCH power. Why? Why do we allow that?

One way to work on our personal power is to change, "Yes, but" to "So what." Multitudes of clients have told me they cannot feel deserving because of their pasts. "Yes, Susan, I believe I deserve, but my mother told me she never wanted me." "Yes, Susan, I know I am special, but being abused has shattered my life. "We need to replace that word "but" which keeps us marinating. SO WHAT that Mom called you stupid...SO WHAT that Grandpa said you would never make something of yourself.

SO WHAT that Dad laughed at you and called you names. This is not to underplay past trauma or treat it as unimportant. Believe me, with practice, saying the "so whats" is incredibly powerful. If you didn't go to college because your mother called you stupid, that is incredibly unfortunate. Doesn't mean you can't sign up for night classes NOW and kick academic butt now. No "yes, buts". Imagine the look on someone's face when you present your diploma! YES YOU...the supposed stupid one! If school is not your thing, cool. Life has thousands of opportunities for us to shine. It is SO important to keep searching for your passion. What will make you happy and proud and powerful? Everyone can be a success!

Another important part of the Law of Attraction and personal power is gratitude. Gratitude is by far one of the most positively-charged emotions there is. Expressing gratitude is like launching one rocket after another into the Universe; good rockets that will yield good results. When I first began reading about the importance of gratitude, I reacted as some of you might, "What do I have to be grateful for?" I would think of less than a handful of things I was blessed to have and piles of stuff that sucked. That was where I was stuck. I began realizing the piles were keeping the negative momentum flowing. Each day (especially morning and evening, which are power times), it is crucial to be mindful of giving gratitude. Each Saturday morning a church down the street offers free breakfast to anyone who walks in the door. Each morning I watch people walk past our house headed for the church. All good, kind people who may not have eaten anything else up until then. And each Oh Happy Day...! morning, I pause and give thanks for my home, my full refrigerator and anything else that comes to mind. Every second of every day gives us the opportunity to be grateful. What we CHOOSE to do with it is up to us.

One challenging aspect of the Law of Attraction is when we THINK we are being positive so often and little good immediately happens. I SO get that! One study concluded we have anywhere from fifty to seventy-five thousand thoughts per day; that's between thirty-five to forty-eight thoughts per minute! Just like homework in school, we need to consistently monitor and be willing to change our thought patterns for the good to come. Think of a swimming pool: when we walk in a circle in the water, the momentum of the water increases. It is so strong that eventually when we stop walking, the water carries us. When we try to turn around, we almost get knocked over by the current. Only by trudging through the water in the reverse do we permit momentum in the other direction. Exactly true about our thoughts; and exactly true about the Law of Attraction. We need to be mindful of our momentum. The truth is every split second of life produces something good; a beautiful sky, a baby's laugh, delicious ice cream, finding money, hearing a funny story, taking another breath....get the message here? GOOD THINGS ARE ALWAYS WITH US. It is our choice to see them or not. To embrace them, or not. And when we do, we are building positive momentum toward good things. When we are in the throes of bad it is so difficult to see good. Now you are learning that we attract it all and the bad will shift if we choose to focus on the good.

Every time a client tells me they "can't," I share this tidbit: Marcus lives where I do; a small shore town in New Jersey. He drives past my home several times a month. When I see him, I smile and wave and say out loud, "I wish you well." And I mean it. I am no braver or better than ANY of you. I do it because I CHOOSE to. I choose to release any and all power he once had over me (key word here: once). I choose to let go of the past and live my life my way. I choose to be happy and free. And you can, too. Think about it.

SOME BOOKS ABOUT THE LAW OF ATTRACTION

Excuse Me, Your Life is Waiting: The Astonishing Power of Feelings, Lynn Grabhorn (Newburyport: Hampton Roads Publishing, 1999)

The Secret, Rhonda Byrne (New York: Atria Books/Beyond Words, 2006)

The Power, Rhonda Byrne (New York: Atria Books, 2010)

The Magic, Rhonda Byrne (New York: Atria Books, 2012)

The Amazing Power of Deliberate Intent, Esther and Jerry Hicks (Carlsbad: Hay House, 2006)

Ask and It Is Given: Learning to Manifest Your Desires, Esther and Jerry Hicks (Carlsbad: Hay House, 2004)

Wishes Fulfilled: Mastering the Art of Manifesting, Dr. Wayne Dyer (Carlsbad: Hay House, 2013)

The Power of Now, Eckhart Tolle (Vancouver: Namaste Publishing, 2004)

Jack Canfield's Key to Living the Law of Attraction: A Simple Guide to Creating the Life of Your Dreams Jack Canfield, (Deerfield Beach: HCI, 2007)

Infinite Possibilities: The Art of Living Your Dreams, Mike Dooley (New York: Atria Books/Beyond Words, 2010)

The Seven Spiritual Laws of the Success: A Practical Guide to the Fulfillment of Your Dreams, Deepak Chopra (Novato: New World Library/Amber-Allen Publishing, 1994)

You Can Heal Your Life, Louise Hay (Carlsbad: Hay House, 1984)

The Alchemist, Paulo Coehlo (New York: Harper Collins, 1993)

ABOUT THE AUTHOR

Susan M. Bisaha, LPC, has been a teacher, school counselor, therapist and Life Coach in private practice for almost twenty-five years. She lives at the Jersey Shore in New Jersey with her wife, Kate and their four furry kids: Lucie, Louie, Stanley and Josephine. Susan is currently in private practice in Allenhurst, NJ.

For an appointment, please email sbisaha@optonline.net

Made in the USA
Middletown, DE
26 June 2018